THE STOCK CAR GHOSTS

THE STORY OF THE 1955 AMERICAN STOCK CAR

TOUR ACROSS ENGLAND

BY STEVE DAILY

This book is raising funds for the Rowans Hospice.

Registered Charity Number 299731

The Rowans Hospice is a local charity providing specialist end of life Hospice care and support to patients with life-limiting and progressive illnesses resident in Portsmouth and South East Hampshire, as well as offering support for their relatives and carers. All care is given without charge.

Although the Charity receives some statutory support from the NHS and Social Services, almost 90% of the money required needs to be fundraised each year. This wouldn't be achieved without help and support from the local community. By purchasing this book, you are helping the charity continue to provide specialist Hospice care to those who need it most.

Thank you.

For more information visit www.rowanshospice.co.uk

Credits and Acknowledgements

First a big hug to my wife Kim for putting up with many hours without me as I have been engrossed within the internet and many racing books. Secondly I'm grateful to David Kipling of oldstox.com for all the help and encouragement, you told me I could write this book, eventually I believed you. Thanks also to Caron and Danny Myers for the additional information, ex-detective Ian for his help on the 1955 Scotland Yard scenario, and Graham Brown for his advice and foreword. Not forgetting Johnny Pugh, Bobby Schuyler and Neil Castles in the States for their help with finding all of those missing pieces. Lastly thank you to all of the people and companies below for allowing their images and photographs to be published.

Keith Barber - Stock Car magazine

Graham Brown

Neil Castles & family

Neil Crookes - oldstox.com

Alan Harris - The Coventry Telegraph

Scott Harrison - The Cornish Guardian

Graeme Hosken – Digger magazine

David Kipling - oldstox.com

Megan Klintworth - The Abraham Lincoln Presidential Library and Museum

Springfield, Illinois

Caron and Danny Myers – oldstox.com

Mike Riata - The International Motorsports Hall of Fame, Lincoln, Alabama

John Teece - oldstox.com

Mark Waldron - The News, Portsmouth

Lyn Wilton

Mark Woodhouse - The Liverpool Echo

CONTENTS

Foreword by Graham Brown

I suppose mine and Steve's routes into oval racing were similar. Like almost everyone, I too started out being taken along by my parents as a kid. They also initially discovered BriSCA stock cars but went on to mainly watch Spedeworth events simply because the Spedeworth tracks were almost on our doorstep.

Thereafter mine and Steve's paths diverged. I would surely have loved to drive myself, but as a teenager I lacked both the money and the facilities necessary. So I got involved by helping other people as a mechanic. Then I got involved in writing about the sport (mostly Hot Rod racing) and have probably penned hundreds of thousands of printed words by now. Most people probably know me as a contributor to the weekly Motorsport News newspaper (I'm their longest serving writer after 46 years) as well as other specialist oval racing magazines.

Later still I became a broadcaster and then got involved in the organisational side of racing. But from around 1968, I started collecting memorabilia associated with the sport, initially programmes but, later on, just about anything – an interest which makes one into an historian almost by default.

I first came across Steve Daily when I purchased a lovely little diorama from him on eBay. The scene featured Superstox at Cross in Hand and was made using Corgi Rockets models; I fell in love with it at first sight and had to have it.

I have since acquired several similar models built by Steve. Perhaps not unreasonably, I started out by assuming he was a long-standing fan and probably a long serving Spedeworth fan too – both of which turned out to be true. But I soon realised that his interests and knowledge extended far beyond events which only took place on the Spedeworth raceways. For a start, many of the dioramas he's constructed are of scenes from the pioneering days of the 1950s, at tracks like Belle Vue and Sheffield, and long before Spedeworth even existed. And the amount of research necessary to get these depictions and the cars in them accurately represented immediately moved Steve from the realm of 'super fan' to that of 'historian' in my eyes. And the more we exchanged emails about various arcane historical happenings, and subjects as diverse as Bernie Ecclestone, Portsmouth and Neath Abbey, the more I realised just how knowledgeable about stock car history he is.

This becomes less of a surprise when you learn that he began going racing at Harringay in 1961! He was immediately hooked by what he describes as "great fun, a cross between motor racing and a circus". The somewhat arduous trek in those days from South to North London was eventually dispensed with when Spedeworth opened up at Wimbledon, thus giving Steve a rare thing in that era; a knowledge of racing on both sides of 'the political divide'.

He went on to race himself, initially in Bangers in the mid-1970s, before progressing to Superstox for a short time - mostly at Ringwood – meaning he has also seen life from both sides of the safety fence.

Given his intense interest in all things stock cars and historical it was, therefore, not much of a shock to me when he started work on researching the once famous but now largely forgotten visit of the Americans in 1955. This was an important and pivotal moment in the UK sport, as it was the flying machines from the USA which really showed the way forward for car development this side of the Atlantic.

I am so pleased that Steve decided to put all of his research into book form, and there is no doubt in my mind that no-one has ever before looked at the tour and everything surrounding it in quite so much detail.

I do hope you enjoy reading the story of the 'White Ghosts' as much as I have.

Graham Brown

Introduction

It was April 28th 2020 here in the UK and like most of the world we were in lockdown due to the Coronavirus that had swept around the planet. Having a personal interest in stock car racing, and while the pandemic progressed, I began to reflect that it was 65 years ago that the stock car fraternity in England were witnessing some of the best drivers and advanced race cars they'd seen to date, on an oval race track.

Maybe we should be reminded just what a draw these Yanks were back then, when Stock car racing was only just beginning a second season in the UK and what a couple of years they were. Huge crowds of spectators flocked to see these crazy guys smashing up their cars whilst trying to race them around in circles, well ovals actually. Sometimes 40,000 or more would be entertained. Drivers were drawn into this motoring circus by the generous prize money on offer and some just for the thrill of it all.

The bubble had burst after two seasons but in the spring of 1955 the Americans arrived at the height of its popularity and raised the bar even further in regards to the competitive opposition.

References to the 1955 tour can be found in original newspapers and programmes and the odd magazine article. Two of the original team members wrote their racing memoirs, devoting a few pages to their recollections of the tour before giving much more detail to the rest of their extensive racing careers. Curtis Crider wrote his story, *The Road to Daytona*, in 1987 some 32 years after the tour. Neil Castles told us his version of events in, *Neil Soapy Castles - Memoir of a Life in NASCAR and the Movies,* in 2019, sixty-four years later. Having read and re-read all of the material I could find on the subject I still found gaps; it was like finishing a jig-saw and finding pieces missing. After emails, phone calls and letters to as far away as America and Australia I now have this, an in depth view from the early days of NASCAR through to the tour of 1955 followed by an account of just what became of the two US managers and the seven team members known by the fans as 'The White Ghosts'.

Bygone US stock car action.

The International Motorsports Hall of Fame

Chapter One – NASCAR

No one can lay claim to inventing the sport of stock car racing, which has its roots in the Southern States of the USA, the Prohibition era, and an unhealthy connection to the transportation of an illegal spirit called moonshine. Being able to out run the local police during the 1930s with 100 gallons of illicit liquor in the back of your car wasn't easy. It called for some specialised tinkering to the suspension as well as the engine and yet to an onlooker the vehicle looked basic or 'stock' to use the American term. Vehicles modified in such a way could carry a full load and still reach speeds in excess of 100 mph.

After WW2 many returning servicemen looking for some excitement would join in at the local stock car races. Anyone finding an old 'hooch hauler' to drive was likely to be very successful. During the early days some race meetings were rough and ready affairs. This applied to the race drivers as well as their cars. After a battle out on the track drivers would often exit their cars and continue the battle on the infield.

The track could be just as basic with a ¼ mile oval marked out in the red clay. Amenities usually included a rickety wooden grandstand for spectators along the start and finish straight. The onlookers protection consisted of a two wire safety fence hung along a row of upright railway sleepers. Along the outside of the back straight would be a tall wooden perimeter fence. This was less of a safety fence and more of a garden fence. Often a race driver would lose control of the car with an involuntary right turn, as his stock car clearly wanted to know what was on the other side of that fence. They would soon find out after leaving a car sized hole in it. The enthusiastic spectators would always go home covered in a liberal sprinkling of dust but they enjoyed every minute.

There is a well know saying that refers to those old style raceways, along the lines of," Dirt is for racing and asphalt is for getting to the track."

At the tail end of 1947 a meeting took place at the Streamline Hotel in Daytona Beach, Florida. Chairman of the proceedings was Bill France who was already the director of the National Championship Stock Car Circuit (NCSCC). This sanctioning body had been founded by Bill himself. The original name, the Stock Car Auto Racing Society was quickly dropped as it spelled out SCARS. Advertised as a convention, it was open to all independent operators and interested parties. The main objective of this meeting was to lay the foundations for a National body that would run stock car racing throughout the US and join up the fragmented sport which could then go forward under one national banner. In February 1948 NASCAR, the National Association for Stock Car Auto Racing, was founded with Bill France as elected President.

NASCAR's first race meeting as the sanctioning body didn't take place until February 15th 1949, some twelve months later. It was for the popular Modified division and ran at Daytona Beach, Florida.

The American Automobile Association (AAA) ran most of the early US motorsports. They had run stock car meetings but their flagship annual event since 1911 was the Indianapolis 500 where the open wheel racers, which later became known as Indy cars, would travel 200 laps around the 2.5 mile rectangular track with four right angled corners each being ¼ mile in length. Smaller brothers to the fold were the Sprint cars which favoured the shorter ½ to ¼ mile oval tracks along with the even smaller Midget race cars. Then there were the other stock car sanctioning bodies, the National Stock Car Racing Association (NSCRA), the United Stock Car Racing Association (USCRA), the National Auto Racing League (NARL), and the American Stock Car Racing Association (ASCRA) and the South Carolina Racing Association (SCRA). So in their first couple of seasons NASCAR had a few rivals.

A typical 1940s back straight and perimeter fence.

The International Motorsports Hall of Fame

Bill France may have had the NASCAR banner created on paper but not everyone wanted to be under it. The last on that list was probably the most painful as his close friend Joe Littlejohn had now defected and started the South Carolina Racing Association in partnership with a certain Buddy Davenport, a name that will crop up again later.

Bill France's vision was that the basic stock car division, known then as Strictly Stock, would feature late model cars as found in any of the main dealer car showrooms. The Modified division would be a support along with a Roadster class. The first part of the plan had to be delayed as there were precious few new cars in the showrooms at that time and the manufacturers were still getting geared up with post war production, supply being out stripped by demand. The Strictly Stock division was, for the time being, open to any full size American car but was yet to show its full potential, some even thought of them as slow and boring. However the Modified division were anything but boring, being typically created from a 1930s sedan with a highly tuned engine and modified suspension. Most were fitted with quick change rear ends and matched gear ratios to the length of each race track. The Modifieds also used special manifolds and multiple carburettors. They were fast, noisy and very popular with the spectators.

Last, and probably least, came the Roadster division for pre-war open top roadsters. These were not popular and proved to be a flop. They were therefore dropped from the menu. Fortunately Bill France had another plan up his sleeve, the Sportsman division.

In August 1949 he advertised the first Sportsman event at the Bowman Gray Stadium in Winston-Salem. Two races would be open to all amateur drivers using cars from 1932 or later with a value not exceeding $600.
Apart from a few adjustments nothing could be modified so they had to use a stock manifold and carburettor. This meant that stock car racing was open to all working class drivers with some mechanical knowledge.

Local farmers or mill workers could have a Ford V8 coupe race car on track for as little as $100. As well as creating an influx of new local drivers these new boys would, in turn, bring along their friends and family members to watch and therefore all pay full admission. A record crowd of 8,000 showed up to see the thirty seven amateur drivers entertain them. The Sportsman division was put onto the NASCAR schedule for 1950.

It was to prove the perfect gateway for an entry into the NASCAR family. Many of the top drivers began their stock car racing careers in the new low-budget Sportsman class.

7

The first NASCAR Strictly Stock race was held at Charlotte Speedway in North Carolina on June 19th 1949 and was a 200 lap race covering 150 miles on the ¾ mile dirt track. The Strictly Stock title changed in 1950 and was rebranded as the Grand National division, being named after the world famous Aintree horse race. The NASCAR Grand National thoroughbreds began to make headway in the popularity stakes.

There is another comparison to horse racing in American stock car racing. Throughout the divisions you will find owner drivers racing on the track but there are a large number of owners and teams that employ their drivers rather like race horse owners and their jockeys. Back then stock car owners could practically adopt their young drivers and they would often eat and sleep under the same roof as their employers.

In the summer of 1950 a new track opened and was ready to slot itself into the NASCAR history books after a bizarre chain of events.

The original Sportsman division launched many NASCAR racing careers.

The International Motorsports Hall of Fame

Peanut farmer, Harold Brasington, had witnessed for himself the Indianapolis 500 race and longed to see a 500 mile stock car race on a similar paved track in the South. There was one problem, that track didn't exist, but Harold had a dream and so mapped out the track in South Carolina. He began to build a unique 1.25 mile paved track with banked corners, exactly half the length of the Indianapolis track. The land at Darlington had been given to him by a local businessman named Sherman Ramsey in exchange for shares in the project. Known as "Harold's Folly" by the locals, the old peanut field began to take shape but a problem arose during construction as Sherman Ramsey's fish pond was at one end of the track and he wasn't going to move it. This resulted in the straights not being parallel and the turns had slightly different dimensions. At speed this would cause drivers a surprise.

On September 4th 1950 Darlington Raceway was to host the first 500 mile long stock car race, the Southern 500, and was NASCAR's first Grand National race on a paved surface. Thanks to the foresight of Harold Brasington, 25,000 people came to see Johnny Mantz in a Plymouth awarded $10,510 for being the first to cross the line after 400 laps.

The following year Buddy Shuman, was picked by the Ford Motor Company to build three new race cars at his workshop in Charlotte NC. Two of the Fords were entered in the 1951 Southern 500 which was won by Herb Thomas in a Hudson Hornet, earning $8,800, considerably less than the previous year's winner. The new Ford driven by Buddy Shuman himself came 3rd and was awarded $1500. The other car, driven by Fireball Roberts, came in 5th, netting a further $910 and rewarding Ford for having faith in the Buddy Shuman and Willie Thompson workshop. Shuman went on to record his only NASCAR Grand National win in 1952 with the first race staged in Canada at Stamford Park, Niagara, Ontario.

With Bill France at the helm of NASCAR the opposition gradually joined them or folded. This in turn meant that they would expand across America and have more control over the racing and the race drivers. Some would come to call France a dictator but from the start he knew that a democratic system of one vote for all within NASCAR would get them nowhere and certainly not achieve his own ambitions for the sport. Stock car racing's original association with unlawful activities such as running moonshine was now rigorously played down by NASCAR as its new image became a key factor in their future cooperation with the American car manufacturers. The fact that a lot of the early race drivers from Junior Johnson to Crawfish Crider had all dabbled in the transit of black-market alcohol at some point was largely ignored and was to be swept under a corporate carpet. Bill France now had a commodity with NASCAR and he was determined to sell it to the nation.

Digger Pugh.

Courtesy of Keith Barber – Stock Car magazine

Chapter Two – Digger Pugh

When he introduced stock car racing to the U.K. in April 1954 Digger Pugh was 51 years old, so, I hear you ask, what happened in those first fifty years? Well plenty as it happens, so buckle up as it's a busy and bumpy adventure.

John Wallace Llewellyn Pugh was born on August 11th 1902 in Kingsthorpe, Northampton, where his father worked in shoe manufacturing and young John was put to work learning the shoe trade with his uncle at the age of ten. In April 1916 at the age of 13 he ran away from home, something he was prone to do at that time, but now he had disappeared and his family feared the worst.

Eighteen months later the family received a letter from him on September 11th 1917. He wrote that he had been on the Western Front fighting in the war and had now joined the recruitment drive for the Australian Imperial Forces. He added that he was now in Melbourne, Australia and enclosed a photograph. He was also working in a munitions factory and was earning £4 a week.

After WW1 he joined a travelling boxing booth and became good enough to turn professional in the flyweight division where he fought under the name of Digger Pugh. His professional fighting career began in 1922 when he was up against Bert 'Snowy' Clack and his first entry into the record books resulted in him being knocked out. He obviously made a quick and complete recovery as the following year he married Hilda Kerr who produced a son, Wallace Pugh.

Digger eventually returned to England and in 1927 he spent some time back in his native Northampton. He was in the UK to fight Dick Corbett at the Alcazar Club in London where he lost on a technical knockout.

He came back to England again in 1928, this time with his wife Hilda. He was here to demonstrate an Australian Speedway bike at High Beech in Essex. Later in Wolverhampton he rode in a broadsiding demonstration and was reported to be the star attraction. Meanwhile his wife Hilda was even busier back in Southampton where she gave birth to a daughter named Heather.

The following year Digger was on the bill at the Wyndham Hall in Plymouth where he fought his last professional boxing match against Billy 'Kid' Hughes on May 5th 1929. After yet another defeat (TKO) Pugh decided to quit the boxing ring for the circus ring. Digger joined up with a troupe of acrobats in Australia and in 1930 he went on tour to appear in London. He had now found something that really appealed to him: show business.

In 1933, after a divorce from his first wife Hilda, he married a ballet dancer, Sheila Smale in Waterford, Ireland. Once Sheila was trained as an acrobat Digger formed The Wallabies. This was an act with a mix of trampoline and ground based acrobatic shows where Digger usually played the clown alongside Sheila and four younger girls. The new troupe left Australia in 1937 to tour throughout Asia before travelling on to perform in the UK.

Sheila gave birth to a son, Johnny Pugh, whist in London during 1938. However in September 1939 war was declared with Germany and they had to make their way back to Australia. Digger arranged to return with the troupe via Italy, performing in Milan and Genoa a couple of months before Italy entered WW2 and joined forces with Germany.

Unperturbed Digger took his Wallabies on tour again in 1941, heading east from Australia to Hawaii via New Zealand. At the end of a six month Hawaiian stay they decided to move on to San Francisco but only taking two of the girls, Beryl Howlett and Heather Pugh. The rest returned home to Australia.

Pip - Dot - Beryl - Digger - Betty - Sheila

The Wallabies embark on their 1937 Asian tour.

Courtesy of Lyn Wilton

The remaining troupe went aboard the S.S.Watsonia and sailed east across the Pacific just nine weeks before the Japanese forces attacked the island.

Once in San Francisco they reformed as The Four Imps. Their nomadic lifestyle throughout the USA and Canada included three months touring with the Cole Bros. Circus. They reached New York in 1942 and joined ENSA to sail in a convoy back to England.

With ENSA (Entertainment National Service Association) the act began entertaining the troops but during 1943 Sheila found time to give birth to a son, Peter Pugh. Digger decided to put down roots in London and bought a house in Hounslow in 1945 where Sheila produced another offspring, a daughter, Carol Pugh. The Wallabies then started a two year run at the famous London Palladium, their finest hour being a Royal Variety Performance before the King and Queen in 1946.

Digger was now expanding his entertainment business as a talent agent. He was sending his acts across the Atlantic to the US of A. One of them being Digger's aerial ballet troupe called The Six Cockatoos. These acts consisted mainly of single females but many of them became brides of US suitors and did not return to the UK. It was whilst travelling in America on a business trip in 1948 that Digger witnessed his first US stock car race meeting.

Unfortunately his marriage wasn't going as well as his business deals and he separated from his wife in 1952. Sheila stayed in America with the children, apart from 14 year old John, who remained with Digger.

In 1953 he announced his engagement to another Sheila, one of his aerial performers named Sheila McMahon. Aerial ballet came with its own risks and in 1952, when performing with a circus on Southsea Common, Sheila McMahon suddenly fell 25 feet and was taken to hospital with cuts and bruises along with four unfortunate members of the audience.

During the autumn of 1953 a liaison with a motor racing journalist would lead to another business opportunity, one that would bring a new form of motor sport to the UK: Stock Car Racing.

Chapter Three – The Thrill of the Century

In 1947 a Chicago auto mechanic and businessman named Andy Granatelli convinced the promoter at Soldier Field, in Chicago, to introduce Hot Rods to the track that was used for midget car racing. Granatelli formed the Hurricane Hot Rod Association to give new drivers a chance of racing experience and fame. The Hot Rods then gave way to stock car racing in 1950 and Granatelli joined the Soldier Field promotion team but he had a reputation for staging racing action by paying certain drivers to cause crashes or even flip their own cars. He once staged a stunt to amaze the spectators whereby a track ambulance suddenly joined in a race. After a few laps the ambulance back door opened and ejected the patient (a dummy of course).

Andy Granatelli was destined for fame himself by becoming the CEO of the STP oil treatment company and eventually winning the Indianapolis 500 race as a race car owner, twice!

Two French entrepreneurs, Andy Dickson and Charley Michaelis, were in Chicago in 1952 looking for acts and displays to bring over to France. They saw the crowds heading for Soldier Field and made a last minute decision to join them to experience an American stock car meeting.

This mix of racing and theatrics brought in huge crowds every week and this was the style of racing the two Frenchmen witnessed that night. Both of them had never seen anything like it and had to bring this new sporting sensation back to Paris.

After searching around for premises and cars Andy Dickson and Charley Michaelis began organising racing at the old and rather run down Buffalo Stadium in Paris in 1953. Although this was not to be authentic American style racing with specialised cars they still advertised it as 'Stock Car Racing'. The large old jalopies that turned up to race were soon spinning and bouncing off each other on a track marked out with straw bales. Fortunately the crowd loved this new form of entertainment and so French stock car racing began to grow in popularity.

Motor racing journalist John Bolster had observed this bizarre new form of motor racing in Paris and tried it for himself. He wrote an article in Autosport magazine about this extraordinary new craze that was happening just across the Channel. Soon afterwards he formed an association with showman, Digger Pugh, with a plan to bring this new crazy sport over to the UK.

Digger first needed a suitable arena with a shale oval track to race the cars on. London had plenty of Speedway tracks; each one was inside a greyhound stadium. The majority of these stadia were owned by the Greyhound Racing Association. John Bolster was to prove a useful advocate when drawing up an agreement with the GRA and with them on board Pugh was in a powerful syndicate. Pugh was now ready to establish a business name, The Stock Car Racing Company.

A meeting in the form of a recruitment drive was immediately advertised at the Hammersmith Town Hall. On the day of the meeting Pugh even had a Ford V8 stock car on display outside. Following a film show of American stock car racing there was a talk by both Digger Pugh and John Bolster to tout for new drivers willing to build their own stock cars and race. About a hundred potential drivers enthusiastically signed up.

The race cars used in American stock car racing were those that the average American family drove, or had been driving, on the roads. However in the UK in 1954 the average working man used public transport and a bicycle or maybe a motor cycle to get around. The middle class family may have owned a motor car but then only one that was of a sensible size. The much bigger motors required for stock car racing would once have been owned by doctors, lawyers, government departments, the American Forces or just the generally well off.

After WW2 fuel duty was increased by the Treasury and so the price of petrol became far more expensive. Therefore larger cars became uneconomical to drive and many nearing the end of their life would be a bargain for the budding stock car racer.

New Cross Stadium was available for the first practice trial on March 17th 1954 and the press were invited along to incite media interest.

Amongst the entries were several future stock car stars meeting for the first time whilst getting used to sliding around on the loose shale surface. Pete Tucker, Jack Wells, Mac MacLean, John Goody and a rather posh and buxom lady, as Pete Tucker once described her, who went by the name of Tanya Crouch. Tanya, the daughter of a surgeon, arrived in her Bentley and soon made her mark as she flew round the track in a stock car as fast as the men. She put her technique down to her Army days, driving through the snow in the Austrian Alps. At one point she lost control and headed onto the infield, scattering the officials. Tanya's car slid across the grass and managed to collect a camera and tripod on the way. Luckily the startled cameraman was nimble enough to jump clear.

Digger still had to sell the new sport to the public and so began an advertising campaign. Posters appeared around the capital and not wishing to understate this new enterprise it was advertised as, "The Thrill of the Century!"

With John Bolster's background in proper motor racing and Digger Pugh's grounding in showbiz and entertainment it's probably not surprising how this new baby turned out after being born in South East London at New Cross Stadium on Good Friday 16th April 1954.

If Pugh had been concerned about whether his new venture would be a success he need not have worried. The opening meeting was a sell out with 26,000 spectators crammed inside the small stadium and many thousands more locked outside two hours before start time. At precisely 7.45 pm on went the floodlights to illuminate the shale track and through the speaker system a drum roll was heard to signify the start of the national anthem. The whole crowd stood in anticipation while the military brass band recording played. Finally the ensuing silence was broken by the roar of the crowd as the cars came into view. One by one they rolled across the ramp, over the greyhound track and onto the shale. The cars lined up for the first 15 lap heat, a mixture of big 1930s jalopies of mainly American origin with the glass removed apart from a few windscreens which were permitted for the first few meetings. Reinforced bumpers were prevalent front and rear and most drivers had been busy with their paint brushes to show off some interesting and colourful paint jobs with a few even painting the wheels and tyres. All cars bore their registered racing numbers and all drivers wore their regulation crash helmets and seat belts.

Ringmaster Digger Pugh opened the show and the cars were soon sent off on their rolling lap. The excitement was rising along with the noise of the revving engines as the flag was waved and the fourteen drivers simultaneously floored their accelerator pedals; a new era had begun.

The racing, a la French style, was embraced by the new fans and the drivers alike with all the action you would expect on the tight 262 yard track, as crashing, bashing, roll overs and general mayhem ensued. Through the noise and dust a commentary from John Bolster and McDonald Hobley frantically tried to convey exactly who was in what position during the race. Bolster and Hobley were well known BBC commentators with Hobley having been voted TV personality of year in 1954. John Bolster was described as delighting the crowds as he was wearing a deer stalker hat, tweed jacket and plus fours.

Digger had done his homework that night. With a capacity crowd he had made money, even after all of the expenses and the big prize money on offer. At the first meeting each race driver received £10 appearance money, a sum total of nearly £500. In addition there was more cash available for the winning drivers in the heats and runners up, and even more for the winner of the Grand Final at £50, followed by £20 for second place and £10 for third. The average wage back then would have been less than £10 a week so a successful driver could be looking at taking home a month's wages.

Digger may have thought that he should be paying out the winners in Francs as the invited team of experienced French drivers, in their white cars, were so fast. In the four 15 lap heats, Frenchman William Camus won the first with Fred Parsons from Peckham winning the second. The third heat was won by John Goody and the fourth by Tanya Crouch. The 20 lap Grand Final was won by the Frenchman Chevalier d'Orgeix, a feat which he was to repeat in the next meeting at New Cross on April 30th.

Press reports were favourable and appeared in all of the national newspapers. Tanya Crouch winning a race was the big media item of note as she was a mere woman! Tanya was no push over and would use that media hype to her own advantage with her various sponsors.

A fortnight later the second meeting took place with another huge crowd but it was clear that Digger Pugh was becoming a victim of his own success as New Cross Stadium was already proving far too small for this exciting new sport.

Chapter Four – The Yanks are coming

After just four meetings at New Cross, Digger arranged with the GRA to move. The new location was across the Thames, at the larger Harringay Stadium. The complex here shared the site with the Harringay Arena which was principally used for ice hockey but could also double up for other attractions. Pugh had originally wanted to use Harringay, not New Cross, but the GRA felt the smaller venue would be less of a risk for the untried and untested sport.

A new show in town was thriving at the Harringay Arena, Billy Graham and evangelism. Billy Graham was filling his side of the complex and did so for three months. His success was due to free admission, a huge choir and the promise of a better way of life. On the down side, his long stay had upset a few thousand local ice hockey fans whose team had been temporarily evicted. It was now Digger's chance to fill the stadium side of the complex.

The first stock car event here was to be on June 5th but just before that went ahead a rival set up, called The Northern Stock Car Racing Company, had been formed organising their own group of drivers and adding an A prefix to their racing numbers to try to avoid any confusion with the southern drivers. They held their first stock car meeting at the Odsal Stadium in Bradford on May 26th 1954 and, cashing in on the publicity of the New Cross meeting, they attracted an estimated crowd of 40,000 with a prize money pay out of almost £1000.

Then the Belle Vue Stadium in Manchester joined in the fun with their drivers having a B prefix against their numbers. Nevertheless the London based Harringay meetings brought in even more clientele where Digger was to be seen running around organising everything, and everyone, whilst wearing his loud Hawaiian-style shirt. The vast number of drivers booking in to race was causing a waiting list and a new driver might wait weeks to race or even turn up as a reserve.

By the summer stock car racing had reached Scotland and Ireland, opening at Motherwell, Edinburgh and Dublin. Every week more and more raceways opened as new promoters began to view the stock car craze as a prospector might have greeted the Klondike Gold Rush. Digger Pugh was following suit and also opening more raceways to the sport.

At this time in motorcycle Speedway racing, using the same premises, things were going through a bad patch and the stock car surge wasn't helping. The Speedway Riders Association (SRA) had told the media that they were not worried but then promptly banned all their members from entering a stock car race. This brought about Speedway riders going undercover and racing stock cars using pseudonyms such as Steve Storm, believed to be the Coventry Bees speedway rider, Charlie New.

Digger Pugh had kicked off the first UK stock car racing season and overall things were looking good. There were now groups of successful 'barnstorming' stock car drivers who would travel the country as professionals making money from the sport at weekends plus several meetings in mid-week. However, by the end of August Digger was about to lose the stock car monopoly that he had built up in London.

The Northern Stock Car Racing Company in association with The Regent Stock Car Company were about to promote racing at the huge Custom House Stadium in West Ham. By now Harringay had settled for racing on Friday nights and so West Ham grabbed the Saturday night spot.

Bentley Boy - Alex Landsborough at Belle Vue.

Courtesy of Neil Crookes – oldstox.com

Their opening meeting was on August 28th 1954 and featured a mix of southern and northern drivers. This attracted around 37,000 spectators. Digger was obviously never keen on his drivers attending the rival West Ham meetings but he saw the advantages in a West Ham vs. Harringay team event as he could then host the money spinning return match.

The very next day, August 29th, at Hednesford Hills Stadium, as it was known then, a dis-used reservoir located some 20 miles north of Birmingham, stock car racing opened and a massive crowd of over 50,000 turned up to watch.

Several motor racing circuit drivers were already enjoying the stock car scene such as Brian Naylor and Cliff Davis, when part time racing driver, Bernie Ecclestone, who had some Formula 2 racing under his belt, entered a West Ham stock car meeting on September 11th 1954. At the time Bernie was selling cars and motor cycles in Bexleyheath and this was to be the bedrock of his future business empire. Tempted by the excitement and prize money he raced an immaculate blue Ford V8, number 499A. Sadly he didn't agree with the driving standards saying that they had a total disregard for other people's property! Bernie also raced at Rayleigh in Essex but his involvement was short lived but, being a good businessman, he was to consider the merits of promoting and he knew the Walker family who were building their own raceway at Neath Abbey in Wales.

Meanwhile Digger Pugh went over to the States to meet with Bill France, the President of NASCAR at Daytona Beach in Florida. They both signed an agreement that launched BASCAR, the British Association for Stock Car Auto Racing. This document now linked Digger Pugh with Bill France to promote stock car racing in Britain under the BASCAR banner. Their logo was virtually the same as the NASCAR one used from 1948-55 with the word National simply exchanged for the word British. It may have looked impressive but, just like NASCAR a few years earlier, if no one else wanted to race under the BASCAR title it was just a piece of paper.

Digger had laid out his plans for the future with Bill France and upon his return the news regarding BASCAR was revealed in the UK press. Shortly after this a headline ran in the weekly publication of Speedway & Stock Car World as, 'American Challenge Coming Next Season'. The article mentioned that Digger Pugh had completed negotiations to bring to Britain a team of Americans for next season. In addition to the team of six, it was hoped that three American women would also compete.

Bill France had deflected Pugh's ambitious tour plan into the path of two South Carolina promoters, Lester Vanadore and Buddy Davenport.

On the international front, October 24th 1954 saw a team of English drivers race against a French team at the Buffalo Stadium in Paris. Thirteen drivers made the trip with Digger in tow as the team manager. England won both the four and six car matches. One week later there was a return match, once again in Paris. This time the English lads complained that their cars, provided by the French team, were absolute rubbish and needless to say, England lost this one as France claimed a victory.

As the season began to wind down so the professional groups of drivers would have to find other jobs, although there were still eight more meetings held in December around the country. As well as those few drivers that have been mentioned so far, other names had been introduced to the fans over the year; Maxie Bacon, Lofty West, Gil Cox, Alan Briggs, Whiskers Woolnough, Harold Bosworth, Wrecker Meadway, Jack Tipping, Bill Bendix, Johnny Brise, Max Glasspole, the Hart family and many more, in fact a cast of thousands, to use a phrase from that classic oval racing movie, Ben Hur!

George Teece (175) makes contact at Rayleigh.

Courtesy of John Teece – oldstox.com

In that first season thirty eight different tracks held 191 meetings and the number of people that came through the turnstiles must have been immense.

During the winter it's estimated that 2,000 drivers were either building new cars or tweaking the old ones for improvements and generally getting ready for the next season to commence.

John Goody and Tanya Crouch officially teamed up in yellow livery and were now sponsored by Picture Post magazine whilst both Johnny Brise and Mac McDonnell spent a small fortune on improving their power output by fitting Ardun kits to their Ford V8's. This kit used aluminium cylinder heads to convert the engine from side valve to overhead valve. The kits would have cost in the region of £200 each at the time.

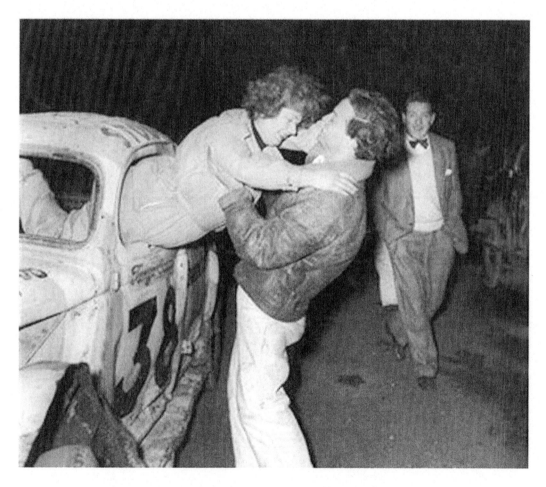

The popular duo of Tanya Crouch and John Goody.

Courtesy of David Kipling – oldstox.com

Come the New Year Digger Pugh started the ball rolling by arranging a reunion dinner and dance event to welcome back all of his race drivers. This was held at the Hammersmith Town Hall on the Wednesday evening of February 16th 1955 and was sold out with 400 guests. The afternoon was taken up with a drivers meeting which proved eventful when one of Digger's co-directors, Jack Wiggins, addressed the drivers and was heckled by some anonymous people in the front row who promptly showed him the door and he was never seen again. This strange incident was talked about afterwards but was never fully explained except to say that Digger must have wanted him gone. The popular dinner, dance and cabaret held that evening was a sensation and of course included one of Digger Pugh's trampolines!

The very next day Digger had to jump onto a plane and fly to New York. This may not have been a pleasant trip for several reasons. Heading west the outgoing flight took 10 hours and 22 minutes as it was against head winds, and stopped for re-fuelling at Newfoundland. By contrast the return journey only took 6 hours and 11 minutes and was a direct flight due to the tail winds. Furthermore, flying at lower altitudes than today, they would have experienced more turbulence and the sick bags were frequently used by the less resilient passengers, and more importantly, it would also have cost an expensive $290 one way.

Once safely on the ground at Idlewild Airport, now known as JFK, Digger went to his favourite haunt, the Schuyler Hotel in Manhattan. Suitably refreshed he left New York and headed south to meet Bill France. Big Bill was 6 feet 5 inches tall and with Digger Pugh being a fraction over 5 feet 1 inch you could hardly call their meeting face to face.

Pugh's trip was to coincide with the Daytona Beach race week. During this meeting of minds Digger also met NASCAR's executive manager Pat Purcell and commissioner 'Cannon Ball' Baker in a room where they were surrounded by 200 trophies ready to be presented to the week's most successful competitors.

The heads of BASCAR and NASCAR signed a new contract, the formation of IASCAR, the International Association of Stock Car Auto Racing, a body to control all stock car racing with Bill France as President and Digger Pugh as vice President. This may have sounded like a powerful alliance but in reality it was practically obsolete as soon as the ink was dry.

Digger had been talking of expanding to Sweden, Belgium, and Spain. He even came up with an ill-conceived scheme to race stock cars in India. All of these plans were, apparently, wishful thinking as nothing ever came of them.

Later that week Digger witnessed the 125 mile mixed Sportsman and Modified race which had a huge line up of 99 cars. Unfortunately during the race there was a two car wreck which resulted in a fire. Jim Thompson escaped with broken bones but Al Briggs died afterwards with 90% burns. This incident was later mentioned in the April 8th Harringay programme notes but is played down by stating that one man was unhurt and the other suffered minor burns.

On the Sunday afternoon the festivities culminated with the big finale, the 106 mile Grand National race. This unfolded as a comfortable win for Fireball Roberts but 24 hours later he was disqualified for having pushrods that were illegally ground and polished. The win was then given to the second man home, Tim Flock. Ironically Tim Flock had actually won the race the previous year but was then disqualified in the same way. So Tim had to wait a year for the win.

Digger rushed off, travelling 400 miles to Greenwood in South Carolina, to meet with the two men who would become the US team managers.

Speedweek at the Daytona Beach and Road track during February 1955.

The International Motorsports Hall of Fame

The tour plans were finalised with Buddy Davenport and Lester Vanadore, the President of Southern Promoters Inc. Vanadore and Davenport ran three popular raceways in Columbia, Rock Hill and Greenwood, all in South Carolina.

The next day, February 28th, Pugh spoke to a local Greenwood reporter. He told him that the deal was done and that six American drivers would be coming over to race at seven tracks in England and Scotland. They would compete against drivers from the UK and France. Pugh went on to say that the two promoters could also make good money putting on their own promotions whilst in the UK. He added that the US drivers should run rings around the British drivers due to their superior cars.

The deal agreed upon by the three must have been lucrative as Southern Promoters Inc. would have to loan out or close their own tracks for several months with the loss of income. What we do know, thanks to Johnny Pugh, is that Digger was footing the bill for the shipping of all the cars and the whole group to sail across the Atlantic on the Cunard liner the Queen Mary.

Once he was satisfied that everything was in place for the tour Digger could return home and would disclose the full details of his trip to the Stock Car Racing Company board.

Vanadore and Davenport had already met with Buddy Shuman and Leland Colvin, the president of Darlington Raceway and a businessman with tobacco warehouses in Darlington, South Carolina. They cut a deal with a view to supplying race cars for the trip, which were to be of the NASCAR Sportsman division. Just how much money was up front and how much was a loan is unknown. Lester Vanadore and Buddy Davenport had until the end of the month before the whole tour team would board the Queen Mary in New York and sail for England.

With Bill France sidestepping the prospect of getting involved with Pugh's tour plans he wished Vanadore and Davenport all the best for the trip. France had made sure that the whole event was unofficial and not connected with him. This explains why there was never any mention of the trip in any official NASCAR paperwork, publications or publicity.

Chapter Five – The Tour arrives in London

Curtis 'Crawfish' Crider received a call from Buddy Davenport to invite him onto the tour. Curtis had a new car ready to go, a '37 Ford coupe with a modified '48 model engine. Davenport agreed to ship it over with the other team cars and then pay him $100 a week (roughly £40) and Curtis could keep all of his prize money. That was a good deal as all the other drivers would only be paid $50 a week as they were driving the team cars. Furthermore they could only keep half of their prize money, the other half being kept by Lester Vanadore and Buddy Davenport.

With Crider agreeing to the terms they now had seven stock cars and drivers lined up for the trip. Five of the team cars, painted white, were all late 1930's (model 78) five window coupes, each one powered by a highly tuned 3.9 litre Mercury Ford V8 engine. Crider's own stock car was left as it was; two-tone blue and cream.

The planned appearance of Speedy Thompson and his car fell through and so a last minute change of plan saw Neil 'Soapy' Castles join the team. With no time to paint the car white, Neil took an insignificant grey '34 Ford (model 40) coupe that was prepared in the workshop. In retrospect this would have suited Buddy Shuman as his young employee could now keep a close eye on the tour and his investment.

Neil had got the name Soapy from his boss, Buddy Shuman. When he was a young lad Neil was caught speeding down the road by the Police in a soap box cart. Curtis Crider was known as Crawfish after he careered off a race track and had to exit his race car in a muddy creek. Another driver, Lewis 'Possum' Jones, was called Possum for his love of sleeping, according to Curtis Crider.

As there were no crew of mechanics going on the trip Crider took control of organising a catalogue of spare parts that ought to be accompanying them and gave it to Buddy Davenport. Once these were obtained the race cars were laden down with an array of parts, new and used, before being loaded onto trucks with their tools, equipment and luggage in Charlotte. Buddy Shuman had supplied most of the spare parts, as well as most of the cars, and had put Neil Castles in charge of keeping tabs on them.

Shuman would charge Lester Vanadore for anything they would use on the tour. Buddy Shuman also told Neil to keep an eye on the race car driven by Bill Irick, number 25, because it belonged to his business associate Leland Colvin.

Lester Vanadore wasn't intending to use a bus or a taxi to get around London. He drove up in a blue Buick convertible and was taking it with him on the trip.

They'd all had the necessary inoculations and their passports were in order. The group going overseas had grown to ten. Lester Vanadore took along his wife Sara with Buddy Davenport, then Curtis Crider, Bill Irick and Bobby Schuyler from South Carolina, Neil Castles and Bobby Myers from North Carolina and Pete Folse and Possum Jones, they had travelled up from Florida.

Unfortunately a last minute hitch had cropped up. One of the truckers assigned to drive to New York had been out partying the night before and was still intoxicated. Neil Castles was asked if he would drive the truck and, when he agreed, the convoy set out on the first stage of their journey with over 600 miles to cover by road in order to reach the Cunard piers in Manhattan.

They arrived in New York the next day, several days before their departure time. Neil remembers that he was making himself useful at the dockside draining fuel out of the stock cars and Vanadore's Buick. This was a standard safety procedure laid down to avoid a fire occurring in the hold of the ship.

Meanwhile back in the UK the first meeting of the season had got going at Belle Vue, Manchester on March 9th 1955. On a freezing cold night all the fans were treated to a great evening's entertainment. John Goody, and Tanya Crouch, had travelled from London and Sussex respectively, to show off their latest bright yellow Picture Post sponsored cars. Then, a few days later, March 12th saw the opening of Neath Abbey raceway in Wales while Digger had opened the next day at Oxford's Cowley Stadium. This was the first chance for Johnny Brise to try out the new Ardun powered stock car and it flew. He won his heat and the Final one lap ahead of second place man, Fred Mitchell.

A fortnight later Digger arranged Speed Trials at Harringay to determine which drivers would be considered fast enough to be in the England team that would be challenging the overseas visitors.

Back in the States, on the Hudson River, the Americans were ready to sail forth on their adventure with their precious cargo now secured inside hold number two on the Queen Mary. A large crowd would usually gather to wave and cheer at the end of the piers when the transatlantic ships left the docks in New York. Thursday March 31st was no exception.

The Queen Mary manifest shows the group of ten American passengers on board, sailing from New York to reach Southampton on Tuesday 5th 1955. They stated on the paperwork that they would be abroad for up to six months except for Bill Irick who seemed to know that three months would be more than adequate. The team were very impressed by travelling on the luxury liner although the fact remained that most of them had never been abroad before.

After five days at sea they stopped briefly at Cherbourg, France and then sailed on overnight to arrive in the early hours at Southampton docks. The Buick and the seven race cars were finally unloaded on the dockside where they were all re-fuelled whilst the team and their two managers met Digger Pugh and his General Manager Peter Arnold along with many other drivers who had come down to meet the American team and transport them, and their cars, the eighty miles to London.

Everyone there wanted to see the American stock cars and were surprised at just how advanced they were. The Sportsman class stock cars were no longer the poor relations compared to the other NASCAR divisions. They'd moved on over the seasons and had most of the available racing modifications on their cars. Quick change rear axles, triple carburettors and a modified chassis were now legitimate accessories and therefore their race cars were perfectly set up to turn left on the track at speed. With this in mind the Americans were very relieved to find out that we raced in the same direction, anti-clockwise.

The American stock cars looked lighter in weight when compared to our ironed up cars and they also had the awesome power of those tuned Ford Mercury V8 units.

Johnny Pugh recalls that before reaching their destination, in North London, the American team convoy got as far as Piccadilly and the lead truck 'broke down' causing an immense traffic jam. Of course this was just a publicity stunt and Digger Pugh had made sure that all of the team cars were flying the Stars & Stripes. After spending enough time there, advertising the team's arrival, the lead truck was suddenly fixed and the journey commenced to Harringay.

Once there the team cars were unloaded and stored in a large workshop in the Harringay Arena complex. Here they could be maintained and kept in working order. Johnny Pugh said that Digger helped Tom Arnold organise the circus at the Arena every winter and Tom had given him the workshop to use while the US team were here.

The ten American visitors found a London still healing and rebuilding a decade after the end of WW2 with many flattened bomb sites still to be found.

The Americans were soon billeted into boarding houses or small hotels in the area. Mr and Mrs Vanadore would have had a hotel room with a phone, keeping them in contact with home and any promoters or stadium owners with a business deal to consider. Most of the drivers shared rooms as they were paying for their own accommodation and saved money that way.

This band of foreigners weren't that alien to us, after all we got to see them enough in the American films shown in the many cinemas around at that time. Each had just one screen back then and a long queue outside waiting for the doors to open. This, in turn, would attract a few medal wearing disabled ex-servicemen from WW2 who would start busking outside for loose change.
We had things in common with the Americans; we both spoke the same language, well very nearly, and it had also been less than two years since we had shared another war together, in Korea. On the down side they had to watch out crossing the road as we all drove on the wrong side! Our currency was to prove yet another unexpected puzzle.

Once they had exchanged dollars, at the 1955 rate of 2.4 dollars to the pound, came the interesting part: change, or to be more precise, shillings and pence. Being used to dealing with quarters, nickels and dimes the Americans were looking at eight unfamiliar coins, from the large looking half crown, down to the tiny farthing. They had to remember that there were 12 pence to the shilling and then 20 shillings to the pound and just forget about Guineas!

Another financial problem appears to be the Exchange Control Act of 1947. Neil Castles recalls them all voting for an official Governor to be in charge of their earnings as individuals could not be paid directly, according to Lester Vanadore, who was now left as paymaster and in charge of the purse strings. This decision is questionable though, the Act was primarily used to limit the amount of money UK residents and companies could take out of the country and controlled by the British Banks and H.M. Customs upon departure.

The first chance the team had to test out their American stock cars came on Thursday, April 7th, the afternoon before their first official race meeting. They practiced on the track in the Harringay Stadium which was empty apart from some BBC personnel who were recording their movements for transmission later that evening.

The guys found it so easy throwing the cars around the shale speedway track and once they saw the TV cameras they all started 'Showboating'. They were cornering three abreast then peeling off, re-joining and generally putting on a display. Full of confidence they went back to their digs. The group got together later that evening and found a television set. They were all able to watch themselves, probably on 'Sportsview', with Peter Dimmock being full of admiration and discussing the next nights England vs USA meeting.

Television sets in 1955 were owned by one third of the population and had only one channel, a situation which was going to change later that year with the new commercial channel ITV starting to broadcast and boosting ownership up to two thirds of the population by 1960.

Digger Pugh was delighted with the publicity they had achieved and promised the team a cut of the gate if they went over 40,000.

Digger Pugh had invested a considerable amount of time and money to get the American team over here but would this gamble now pay off and be good enough to draw in the crowds on Good Friday?

Friday April 8th – Harringay – England vs USA International

Even the Americans must have been amazed when a huge crowd of 43,000 jammed into the stadium to cheer on the teams. It was Easter and Good Friday, one year on from the first meeting at New Cross. The race programme listed all of the USA team but included Speedy Thompson rather than Neil Castles. Speedy Thompson had initially agreed to go but then he fell out with Lester Vanadore. Another change was that Neil Castles would now be the new reserve driver rather than Bobby Schuyler. This meant that Neil's real potential wasn't unleashed until later in the tour.

The meeting got underway under the floodlights at 8 pm with the first two racing heats being won by Tanya Crouch and Vince Jones, an American who wasn't connected to the tour. This was followed by a fanfare welcoming both teams onto the track for the very first England v USA International match race. Five points would be awarded for first place down to one point for fifth place.

The teams were, Jimmy 'Whiskers' Woolnough (Captain), John Darrell, Sid Leach, John Goody, Wilbur Chandler, George Teece and reserve Les Pollard for England, all cars flying the Union flag rather than the flag of Saint George. Then Crawfish Crider (Captain), Possum Jones, Bobby Myers, Bill Irick, Pete Folse, Bobby Schuyler and reserve Neil Castles for the USA team with all of their race cars flying the Stars & Stripes.

A coin toss decided that the Americans would have the inside line as Digger Pugh took control, lining up the twelve cars. The tension rose as they set off on their rolling lap and then, as they approached, Digger enthusiastically waved the flag to start the long awaited 20 lap race.

Pete Folse soon retired with a duff engine but the rest of the team were flying. The USA team had shot off and were soon way ahead of the English drivers.

They weren't even slowing down for the corners. At the end of the straights they were drifting almost sideways whilst steering to the right in a perfect arc. The USA team were five laps ahead at the end and won by 15 points to nil.

Result; 1st Bobby Myers USA, 2nd Crawfish Crider USA,

3rd Possum Jones USA, 4th Bill Irick USA, 5th Bobby Schuyler USA.

Being the winning team all seven Americans qualified for the Final. The result had surprised and disappointed the crowd. Even with home advantage the English lads were under powered and being out manoeuvred by those Yanks.

After heat 3, won by the Irishman Phil O'Shea, it was time for the Grand Final. This began with the USA white cars now targets to be aimed at. Every white USA car, along with Crider's, was taken out and failed to finish. But there was a flaw in their plan. They had all overlooked the insignificant looking grey Ford coupe which went on to win the race. Many assumed that Neil Castles had won but, in fact, it was Possum Jones who was driving. The team had put him into the grey car and Neil Castles had driven the white car of Possum Jones.

Grand Final result; 1st Possum Jones USA, 2nd Jack Wells, 3rd Jack Crawley.

George Teece and Curtis Crider racing at Harringay

Courtesy of Keith Barber – Stock Car magazine

Pathe News filmed the highlights to show with their weekly newsreels in the cinemas. The end result was a short clip for posterity, now on YouTube, although it focuses more on Tanya Crouch (38) than any of the American team.

The victorious American team at Harringay

Courtesy of Keith Barber – Stock Car magazine

The show had finished and that was just the first one. Lester Vanadore was heard to say, "Some of the boys got a little sore at being pushed around but they'll settle down okay." Apart from being sore in the English sense they were obviously unhappy with their rough treatment out on the track.

The next day Vanadore and Davenport went to see Digger and took Curtis Crider as a spokesman for the drivers. Digger had prepared the money due to them but then Crider reminded him of the large bonus that he had promised the US team, due to the huge crowd attending the meeting. Digger looked slightly surprised and asked if he had that in writing. He refused to pay them anything above the original contract as if it were just some misunderstanding. Curtis Crider was annoyed but he knew there was nothing he could do about it, as Pugh had reminded him, they had nothing in writing. As far as Curtis Crider was concerned Digger Pugh had got one over on them.

Sunday April 10th – Arlington raceway, Eastbourne.

The next meeting was just two days later at the Arlington raceway. This was a well-publicised affair as it was Diggers first promotion at the track and a new sport to the locals. With its location on the edge of Arlington village in East Sussex it is some ten miles away from Eastbourne.

It was a fine day and as you might expect masses of people made their way to the rural track blocking the lanes for miles in all directions. Improvements before the meeting meant that the small raceway could now accommodate 12,000 paying guests and that was soon reached. The start was delayed to squeeze the last few hundred through the turn-stiles. It was another full house for Digger Pugh. Then people began to climb trees to see inside. Several sitting on top of the Speedway clubhouse roof had a narrow escape when it collapsed.

The local press had been primed by Pugh in advance and had reported the US team's arrival and they had been expecting six Americans to arrive but only three travelled down, Bill Irick, Curtis Crider and Bobby Myers.

Not wishing to see a 1-2-3 American finish, as at Harringay, Digger put one US driver into each of the heats and was again in great form, enthusiastically waving the flags.

Heat one saw local man, Jack Appleby, abandon his upturned car in the middle of the track while Curtis Crider quickly raced round for an easy win with that local Sussex driver of Tanya Crouch in second place. Heat two was another lively race but still won easily by Bobby Myers from John Goody in second.

Heat three was to see a change in fortunes with Johnny Brise unleashing his powerful Ardun Ford V8 motor against that of Bill Irick. The Brise car shot into the lead and stayed there. Even with cars turning over and a complete somersault from one, Brise kept hold of the lead, avoiding the wrecks, and lapped everyone including the American Bill Irick, who finished the race in second place.

After a consolation race, won by Don Busby, there came the Grand Final. The three Americans were up against Tanya Crouch, John Goody and Johnny Brise as the main players and after the flag dropped Crider shot into a good lead once again. Bobby Myers was having trouble with the local boys and got tangled while Tanya Crouch and John Goody were having their own race. Meanwhile Bill Irick's car hit an unexpected problem when his fuel tank fell out and he began towing it behind him before retiring from the race. Johnny Brise and Bobby Myers were having a good battle for second, Myers having caught up to sit behind the Brise car before managing to overtake him.

Result; 1st Curtis Crider USA, 2nd Bobby Myers USA, 3rd Johnny Brise.

THRILL-A-MINUTE STOCK CAR RACING was the title of the enthusiastic report that ran in the local Eastbourne Gazette, whilst toasting the American team.

Back at Harringay again and this time there was a switch to a Saturday night. This meeting was to determine the qualifiers for the Television Trophy race which would be held there the following week. The BBC would be televising the main trophy event with a live broadcast at Harringay on April 23rd. It would be the first stock car race shown on British television. This was to be another feather in Digger Pugh's cap but it was a close run thing as he was nearly beaten to it by his rivals. On Wednesday March 30th, at the Belle Vue Stadium in Manchester, they had made arrangements to bring in the BBC cameras for a live broadcast. They were thwarted when the technicians decided that they should postpone the programme until lighter nights and better weather.

Saturday April 16th – Harringay - TV Trophy - Qualifying heats

The Harringay meeting was to include a team race between Essex and Middlesex in which Essex would manage a win, nine points to six. Heat one was a tame affair and a straightforward win for George Baily. In heat two Cliff May held up Bobby Myers early on and Myers had to make up the distance during the race. Johnny Brise had got off to a flyer with Curtis Crider behind him, eventually Crider got by for the win with Johnny Brise a close second and Bobby Myers catching up for third place ahead of Possum Jones.

Heat three heard a cheer go up when Sid Leach put Pete Folse out of the race until fellow American Bill Irick returned the favour by turning over Leach's car. Bill Irick was then, in turn, spun onto the infield by Steppy Stepenovic. Bobby Schuyler won the race from second place Irishman Pat O'Shea with Irick, the other American, recovering some lost ground and finishing in third place.

The Grand Final was to be yet another American show but this time Johnny Brise was out there to even things up for the home fans. Bobby Myers was putting in quick laps with some perfectly controlled drifting around the bends and had gained the lead by lap eight. There was no stopping Myers and he claimed a comfortable win. However Johnny Brise just out-drove everybody else out there to get a well-deserved second place and stayed ahead of Crawfish Crider and Possum Jones.

Result; 1st Bobby Myers USA, 2nd Johnny Brise,

3rd Curtis Crider USA, 4th Possum Jones USA.

Johnny Pugh said that he can still remember, to this day, the excitement of being a sixteen year old lad and him being allowed to drive one of those powerful American team cars around the empty track after the meeting.

Pete Folse was now the only US team member not to qualify as his car had sustained a broken king pin during heat three. This meant that he would be unable to take part in the following week's Television Trophy.

Chapter Six – Television

Johnny Brise got on well with the American visitors and his was the only race car that could be described as on par with theirs. He took them all down to his farm and showed them around. Curtis Crider never forgot this hospitality and they got on well, so well that Johnny arranged to get Curtis Crider and his car up to a race meeting at Belle Vue in Manchester. Curtis was a member of Vanadore's American tour team but as he had his own car here he didn't see why he shouldn't go off, given the opportunity, and earn himself some extra cash independently, so he agreed to embark on the 400 mile round trip.

The Belle Vue promoter Johnny Hoskins was reputed to be paying Tanya Crouch £50 for appearance money, so it would seem likely that a similar deal was put to Johnny Brise and Curtis Crider.

Wednesday April 20th - Belle Vue Stadium, Manchester.

Heat one got under way with local driver Brian Lennard getting the win ahead of second place man 'Ginger' Holtby. Heat two was Crider's chance to show the crowd just what the American car was capable of and drove at a very fast pace to get the win. He was followed home in second place by local man Harry Kayley. Heat three was all Johnny Brise with another fast and capable drive to collect the race win from the second man to get over the line, Ian Williams.

After the Consolation race, won by David Ross, it was time for the Final. Just which of the two fastest stock cars on the track would win this one? The crowd were in for a treat as the race started and the pace increased. These two aces, Brise and Crider, were flying round one behind the other whilst weaving to and fro around the opposition lap after lap. Scotsman Ian Hastie did his best to take Crider out but failed. A few feet separated the two when the chequered flag was waved at the finish line.

Result; 1st Curtis Crider USA, 2nd Johnny Brise, 3rd Brian Lennard.

This had been a classic battle, a master class in racing between two fast drivers, and the kind of race that takes your breath away just watching.

Just how excited Lester Vanadore got when his maverick driver returned victorious, with a bundle of cash in his pocket, is anyone's guess but I suspect that he was not very happy as he thought he had total control of his team and was paying Crider $100 a week to be in that team. Curtis Crider however saw himself as his own boss as he had his own car so why shouldn't he make his own deals and be more independent of Lester Vanadore and the U.S. team? This successful outing may have sown the seeds of discontent between them as Curtis Crawfish Crider had received his big cash pay-out without having to go through Lester Vanadore.

Saturday April 23rd 1955 – Harringay – The TV Trophy.

With the BBC technicians giving the go ahead all was ready for the first live television coverage of stock car racing in the UK. The programme schedule for that night in the Radio Times was shown as, STOCK CAR RACING 8.45 pm until 9.15 pm, which must have raised a few elderly grey eyebrows among the potential viewing audience.

The Harringay programme notes began with news of their next meeting, 'England v USA Return. Our Chance for Revenge Here on May 7th,' ran the headline. There was also an introduction to an actress, the fair Sabrina, who would be presenting the trophy fresh from her starring role in the Arthur Askey TV show where, I suspect, she raised a few more elderly grey eyebrows!

Pete Folse surveys the damage at the Harringay qualifying night on April 16th.

Courtesy of Keith Barber – Stock Car magazine

The American team were now sporting some proper bumpers and were getting used to our more robust approach to racing. Heat one saw Bill Kennet win from Sid Leach in a rather easy and quiet race. Heat two got Mac McDonnell over the line first from second place man George Methley in another fairly straightforward affair.

Heat three was to be shown on the television and commentator McDonald Hobley asked for some more action to liven things up. He need not have worried, Tanya Crouch was out there. As the race started Bill Buisson and Tom Ryder crashed on the first bend in front of the television cameras. Tanya Crouch decided to turn over the car of Gillian Gill and then spun four more. Then Southampton's Gerry Dommett and Danny Hunt both found themselves inverted. Tanya went on to win the race in some style ahead of her Picture Post team mate John Goody.

It had been a timed race so that they could start the main Television Trophy event on cue; this race would also be limited by the amount of air time left.

The 22 qualifiers lined up with five Americans near the front of the grid along with Johnny Brise. They were soon under way but the threat posed by Brise was quickly nullified when he was put into the fence and then hit by several other cars. The Americans were soon in front as usual and stayed there as the time gradually ran out. Finally the chequered flag dropped and the winner of the Television Trophy was Bobby Myers, ahead of his team mate Possum Jones.

Result; 1st Bobby Myers USA, 2nd Possum Jones USA.

Sabrina, awarded Bobby Myers with the Television Trophy and she was given a big kiss in return, much to the astonishment of the officials who looked on horrified as if lips seen meeting in public was banned under the law.

The evening ended with the Grand Final which had 19 cars lined up with trophy winner Myers at the rear. As soon as the flag dropped he was clearly after another win and began carving through the field. Bobby Myers actually got into first place and had built up a good lead when Allen Briggs had other ideas and spun him out, causing the biggest cheer of the night from the not so impartial crowd! Myers recovered quickly and grabbed second spot behind Possum Jones, who had raced in the grey Neil Castles reserve car yet again.

Final result; 1st Possum Jones USA, 2nd Bobby Myers USA.

Possum Jones had won the Grand Final leaving Bobby Myers to make do with second spot but Bobby Myers had won the Television Trophy and both had finished with a large wad of prize money; half of course, was kept by the US team managers, Lester Vanadore and Buddy Davenport.

Bobby Myers was a bit put out by the looks he got after grabbing a quick kiss off of the young starlet Sabrina, after all that's what you did back home after winning a big race. Bobby's view on the moral code here at the time, which to him looked a bit straight laced, was pretty much correct.

In 1954 the Conservative Government had been worried about us going into a moral decline so they got the artist Donald McGill fined for violating the obscenity laws. His crime was that he had produced most of the saucy seaside postcards for generations, using innuendo similar to that of the 'Carry On' humour. The police were sent out on a shopping expedition. They'd check card owners stock and then confiscate all postcards that were deemed, to them, to be indecent. Eventually though, we found the 'Swinging Sixties' and made up for lost time!

The visitors had now been in the UK for three weeks and were finding their way around. Food rationing had finished one year earlier in 1954 and leaving anything on your plate would be deemed wasteful and frowned upon. Just how the Americans got on with our unfamiliar 1950s English cuisine I can't imagine. The only take-away food would be at the traditional fish and chip shop, there being no Hamburger Diners or Hot Dog street vendors to be found. Although Neil Castles did confess to partaking in the speciality served at the local Café - Egg and Chips!

Possum Jones driving the grey Neil Castles car to victory.

Courtesy of Keith Barber – Stock Car magazine

They would also find that on a Sunday virtually everything was shut due to the Lord's Day Observance Society enforcing the law in 1831 and stopping all Sunday trading. In 1932 the Entertainment Act enabled people to visit the cinema, zoo, museum or picture galley but not the theatre, which remained technically illegal for another 40 years.

In 1954 Donald Martindale, Ron Hart and Oliver Hart were fined £25 each and ordered to share costs of 12 Guineas for promoting a stock car race meeting near Preston on a Sunday under the Sunday Observance Act of 1780. The court considered that charging admission was trading. Other promoters came under threat with an ecclesiastical hand grenade from the Lord's Day Observance Society including Claude Roe at Hednesford in 1955. He felt the sport was being singled out as motor racing and speedway had been racing on Sundays for many years. The maximum fine if found guilty was £100 plus costs.

The next meeting on the tour was to be at Southampton on April 29th but things were about to take an unexpected turn for American visitors.

Digger Pugh had been asking if Curtis Crider would be interested in selling his car to him and in return he could still drive it, win races and share the prize money with Pugh. Curtis spoke to Bobby Myers about Pugh's scheme and found out that Bobby was homesick. A few days after the televised Harringay meeting Curtis spoke to Digger, who must have rated the car highly, as he agreed to buy it for $3,500, roughly £1,400.

SOUTHAMPTON STADIUM

STOCK CAR RACING

RETURNS TO THIS STADIUM ON

FRIDAY NEXT, APRIL 29th, 7.30 p.m.

with

"DIGGER" PUGH'S PICK OF THE AMERICAN ACES

BETTER THAN EVER ----- YOU'LL SEE

Grand Stand : Reserved 10/- Unreserved 7/6

County Stand 5/- Terraces 3/-

Image courtesy of The News, Portsmouth

Digger had time to have an advert published in the Cornish Guardian newspaper on April 28th stating that the May 5th Plymouth meeting would include the American team members, the winner of the Television Trophy, and the much travelled John Goody and Tanya Crouch. He also had time to mention the two Americans in the Plymouth race programme. Clearly Pugh was taking the best two drivers away from Vanadore and Davenport. At the same time Vanadore had already fallen out with Pugh over the next Harringay meeting.

Digger Pugh knew the fans were not impressed with the first dual between the teams as it was so one sided and the advertised international re-match between the two teams, for May 7th at Harringay, never went ahead. At this point you have to remember that Pugh was a successful showman and thought of these events as putting on a show to entertain the public. It's thought that Digger Pugh wanted Vanadore to slow down his team members and allow the US team to 'throw' the match so that England could claim a victory. Looking at the bigger picture this would have left the door wide open for a third tie-breaker contest between the two teams and surely another bumper crowd at Harringay for Digger Pugh.

Lester Vanadore was uncomfortable with Pugh's expectations of him and refused to play Pugh's underhand games. He considered that he had better offers lined up and so cancelled the second England v USA clash at Harringay. The dynamic duo of Lester Vanadore and Buddy Davenport would be moving on elsewhere. Since arriving here Vanadore had received propositions from various promoters around the country who wished to see the American team at their venue. Apart from Crawfish Crider's lone visit to Belle Vue in Manchester, they had so far, stuck with Digger Pugh.

The Americans had been away for just under a month of their three month tour and Crider was already unhappy with the team set up, wishing to make his own plans whilst Bobby Myers wanted to join Crider and shorten his stay rather than looking at the prospect of two more months travelling around the UK with Lester Vanadore and the US team.

The meeting at Southampton was to be the last one on the London based team agenda as the marriage between the three promoters was coming to an end. Vanadore and Davenport were going to head for the Midlands where they would be linking up with Les Marshall in Birmingham.

Not all of the team were going to Southampton, advertised as 'Digger Pugh's pick of the American Aces'. Obviously he'd picked Curtis Crider and Bobby Myers and they were joined by Pete Folse and Possum Jones.

FRIDAY April 29th – Southampton Stadium.

This was the opening meeting of the season at the Bannister Court Stadium in Southampton and Digger Pugh had been advertising it in the local newspapers. Heat one was to include the Americans, Curtis Crider and Pete Folse, the oldest member of the US team. Folse totally out classed the field. Unfortunately Crider spun coming out of the first bend and was involved in a two car collision putting him out of the race. Pete Folse went on to win the heat from two local drivers, Arthur Haines from Warsash and Jack Davies of Swanwick.

Removing the Crawfish Crider car caused a delay, dealing with his small lake of sump oil running across the track. Crider's car was loaded up for the trip back to London with Crider now out of the meeting.

Heat two began with Possum Jones getting an early lead before being challenged by Mac McDonnell and Johnny Brise. Bobby Myers was entertaining the crowd with his long broadsiding around the bends, going faster each time until he over cooked things coming out of the pit bend and crashed into the safety fence. Possum Jones drove on to get the win ahead of Mac McDonnell who was followed home by Johnny Brise.

Then the challenge match, England v USA, in which Sid Leach raced for the USA in his own car in place of the retired Curtis Crider. The visitors showed their advantage once more by taking the first three places.

Result; 1st Possum Jones USA, 2nd Bobby Myers USA,

3rd Pete Folse USA, 4th Reg Beer, 5th Frank Harris, 6th Sid Leach USA.

In the Grand Final Mac McDonnell and Johnny Brise were duelling for the lead as soon as the flag dropped. Brise pulled ahead and got away only to get a puncture. That left Mac McDonnell to fend off the American challenge from Pete Folse who got past, gaining the lead for the last few laps, and the win.

Result; 1st Pete Folse USA, 2nd Mac McDonnell,

3rd Gill Cox, 4th Jack Davies, 5th Possum Jones USA.

Curtis Crider's car was a mess and after a quick look at the damage it was clear he'd need a few parts including a radiator, sump pan, two water pumps plus engine mountings. Yes, these old Ford V8 engines had two water pumps, a left hand and a right hand, mounted on the front, to which the front engine mountings were attached. Curtis had the stock car dropped off at a service station in London with a scrap yard at the rear. He had an arrangement with the owner to keep his car there and repair it before Pugh would collect it.

After obtaining all of the required parts, and with all of them in place, Curtis tried to fire up the engine. The horrible noise that was heard signalled to him that something more dramatic had happened and a depressing conclusion began to sink in. Thinking back to the incident he remembered coming out of the first bend, tangling slightly with another car and spinning around.

Starting near the front of the grid at the beginning of a race is an advantage up until you get spun and have most of the opposition coming towards you, as in this case. A bonus system was operating at the time whereby if you caused the biggest wreck at the meeting you would be awarded £10 and the guy heading his way was clearly after it. Curtis had time to select reverse gear and then floor the accelerator and move backwards to lessen the inevitable impact.

The crash had destroyed the radiator and ripped the engine off of its mountings, which then dropped onto the cross member and crushed the sump against the crankshaft. This, in turn, tore a chunk out of both the sump and the cross member. The stress had broken the crankshaft. This was no ordinary crank; the nearest workshop to stock it was in New York. You can bring along all the parts imaginable but there's always something you don't have in the spares box which left Curtis Crider over 4,000 miles from home with a terminally broken stock car.

He was now facing a dilemma; if he told Digger Pugh the race car had no usable engine he wouldn't get the money but if he fleeced Pugh he would have to get away and go home as soon as possible. Both Bobby Myers and Curtis Crider felt that they had no choice and so agreed to take the money and run!

Pugh's advert published on April 28th 1955.

Image courtesy of The Cornish Guardian

Crawfish Crider figured that Digger Pugh had done them all out of a bonus at the first meeting so he was just getting even and Bobby Myers just wanted to go home. The US team managers, Vanadore and Davenport, knew just what Crider was up to but, as he wanted to leave the team and his car was finished anyway, they didn't really care. What they hadn't bargained for was Bobby Myers leaving the team with him.

Curtis Crider and Bobby Myers had arranged to meet Pugh on the service station forecourt on Wednesday May 4th. Crider says that he took the battery out of the race car and gave it to a man passing with a bicycle, placing it in the basket for him. That small act of charity neatly prevented any easy check on whether the car actually ran or not.

The two drivers had been busy checking their escape route and booked two tickets for the Cunard ship Britannic leaving Liverpool for New York in two days' time. Bobby Myers had left his Television Trophy with Bill Cook for safe keeping but now he would have to leave it behind.

Digger turned up in his Jaguar along with a driver in a truck with a trailer. Crider explained that the battery had been damaged in the accident at Southampton and so the car couldn't be started. This took Digger off guard and so Bobby, Curtis and the driver pushed the car onto the trailer. Then they all went to Diggers house in Hounslow and Crider got his money, $3,500 cash (£1,400). Obviously Digger Pugh had some spare currency under the mattress to invest in the stock car. So far so good but Digger now expected them to travel on to Plymouth.

They both took the local tube to Paddington Station where they would have caught the Plymouth train. Crider and Myers thought that Digger had got suspicions about his unchecked race car and they wanted to go through the motions of their supposed travel plan for Plymouth just in case they were being watched. A wise decision as it happened; Digger Pugh was already at the station awaiting their arrival. Once they saw him they had no choice but to buy two railway tickets to Plymouth. Pugh then kindly accompanied them to their compartment and then stood on the platform to watch them leave. Digger wasn't taking any chances with his investment and was getting the car checked out whilst, at the same time, checking out the two Americans.

The train eventually stopped at Reading. They had travelled 40 miles in the wrong direction, so they got off, bought two more tickets, and waited for the Paddington train. Once they were back where they'd started, in London, they had to get across to Euston Station to buy more railway tickets. By now it was getting late and they were told that there was no direct train service to

Liverpool until the early hours of the morning unless they changed en route. Worried that Pugh was out looking for them they jumped on the next train north. They were both travelling light, looking as if they were on an overnight stay at Plymouth. They were, in fact, going on a sea voyage without any luggage. With the sale of his stock car, Crider was the only one with any money left, mostly Pugh's money.

Pugh wasn't silly enough to take the car anywhere without getting it looked over. As soon as the problem came to light he was venting his anger at the Metropolitan Police. They would only have to check Southampton or Liverpool for transatlantic bookings to New York to find the two culprits.

Thursday May 5th – Having arrived by train earlier in the day Bobby Myers and Curtis Crider had reached the customs area at Liverpool docks and, about to board the Britannic, they felt relieved. This elation was short lived as, when they opened their passport to the customs official, Crider and Myers were summoned to see a man from Scotland Yard. The man in question was accompanied by another, probably from the local Liverpool Police. Crider could only tell them that Pugh bought his car and, if sold as seen applied, it should be O.K. unless, of course, Digger Pugh had trumped up even more charges against them?

Curtis Crider remembered quite distinctly what was said to him. "A man is trying to stop you two from going home," he said, then after a long pause, "We know this man too. He hasn't any case against you so you boys go ahead, get on that ship and go home and good luck to you". Scotland Yard had brought the incident to a quick conclusion. In other words, make sure they both leave the country and 'case closed'. Crider and Myers couldn't believe their luck.

Indeed they did know this man John W.L. Pugh as he had been arrested by Special Branch officers on the liner Queen Elizabeth after it docked at Southampton in 1953. Pugh appeared at Bow Street Magistrates Court in August of '53 accused of falsifying statements for the purposes of procuring passports for four of his aerial ballet troupe. Pugh was found guilty on all four counts and fined £100 plus 10 Guineas costs.

Chapter Seven – To the Midlands and Beyond

Once Digger Pugh knew he'd been double crossed by Curtis Crider the reality of the situation began to sink in. The American team were planning to leave after he had paid for them all to be here plus his attempt to keep two of the American drivers with him, and salvage some respect, had failed. He was also the proud owner of an American stock car with a broken engine for which he had handed over a substantial amount of money. He now felt his generosity had been taken advantage of. He had even invited the whole of the American team to his home for dinner on a couple of occasions since they had arrived.

Neil Castles recalled going to Digger Pugh's house on one of those dinner dates one afternoon and finding a group of acrobats in the back garden. They had a large trampoline and even a high-wire strung out between two buildings. Apparently they would be there several times a week just practicing. He went on to say that the inside of Digger's house was used for storing all kinds of circus related paraphernalia including an array of trapeze equipment.

Digger Pugh decided to put a spanner in the works of those two ungrateful American promoters, Lester Vanadore and Buddy Davenport. Johnny Pugh remembers his father organised a trip to the Harringay workshop and confiscated the six remaining race cars. He then had them all brought back to his house in Hounslow and lined them up along the driveway. It didn't take long for Vanadore to work out where his cars may have gone and so the leafy quiet avenue of Alexandra Gardens was set for a battle of wills. Digger was purposefully trying to make things as awkward as possible for the remaining US team as they were due to race in Birmingham on Saturday May 7th instead of Harringay.

Lester Vanadore had to hire transport to get the team up to Birmingham. Johnny Pugh recalls being at home and at around midnight several trucks and trailers began to arrive. Eventually all of Vanadore's transport was there, parked along the road outside. Then the police appeared with Lester Vanadore. Digger Pugh was told that Lester Vanadore had the relevant paperwork showing that all of the vehicles belonged to him; therefore he had no right to keep them.

A dialogue ensued between Vanadore and Pugh as the cars were wheeled off of the drive one by one and loaded up outside. All the trucks were ready to roll in the early hours and the convoy left to begin their 126 mile journey and meet up with the Midlands promoter, Les Marshall. They had left behind, the still smouldering, Digger Pugh. Johnny Pugh told me that Digger did get an explanation from the Metropolitan Police as to why they had let Bobby Myers and Curtis Crider go home; Crider had kept a receipt for the sale of his car.

Crawfish Crider had now left the team but with Myers accompanying him it must have been a surprise for Lester Vanadore as Bobby Myers was printed in the Perry Barr team line up. The team were now down to five drivers so Buddy Davenport, aged 37, volunteered to be their sixth driver. All remaining team members were to surrender their passports to Buddy Davenport and Lester Vanadore for "safe keeping". The two team managers couldn't afford for any further team members to go missing.

Neil Castles said that the team were booked into a hotel in a town outside of Birmingham which had a large USAF base nearby. They were able to garage the cars by the hotel and soon got to meet several of the Americans from the air base which was a few miles away.

Image courtesy of The Coventry Telegraph

Saturday May 7th – Perry Barr, Birmingham

Races run at Perry Barr were timed at six minutes and the Final at eight. A large crowd watched heat one only to see Neil Castles and Possum Jones as non-finishers and a win for Max Huiss followed by Jimmy Wright from Banbury. Heat two had Bill Irick and Pete Folse as contenders but only Pete Folse was to manage a third place after a tough race that was won by Steve Storm ahead of Robbie Robins in second. Heat three saw Possum Jones qualify with a 5th place using the Bobby Myers car. The winner was Tom Vernall from Ron Griffiths then Reg Spooner in third. The Consolation race was won by Tatter Meadway from Wrecker Meadway and Gordon Saywood.

The 20 car Final was to be the Sabrina Trophy presented by Sabrina herself. Possum Jones was once again driving the Myers car and drove a superb lightning fast race to win the trophy ahead of Steve Storm.

Result; 1st Possum Jones USA, 2nd Steve Storm,

3rd Reg Spooner, 4th Ron Griffiths, 5th Tatter Meadway.

Thousands seek thrills and spills at Perry Barr, Birmingham.

Courtesy of Keith Barber – Stock Car magazine

The sixth meeting of the tour had got off to a shaky start for the Americans with no winners in the heats. But then Possum Jones saved the day by winning the Final, the Sabrina Trophy. On a more positive note Neil Castles would now get into the driving seat more often.

The first week in May was fine and sunny but that was all about to change. The rain was arriving and so the May climate skipped straight from spring to late autumn, the weather was deteriorating.

Meanwhile back in Liverpool the two runaways, Bobby Myers and Curtis Crider, instead of sailing away to New York, were still stuck at the dockside on the Britannic. This delay was courtesy of the Liverpool tugboat crews who had gone on strike. The docks were paralysed with ships queuing along the Mersey. On Wednesday May 11th, after five days on board the Britannic, they were encouraged to take a train down to Southampton and catch another Cunard ship. The next day that ship, the Queen Elizabeth, sailed out of Southampton docks bound for New York with Curtis Crider and Bobby Myers safely aboard and finally heading home.

Friday May 13th – Stanley Stadium, Liverpool.

Lester Vanadore and Buddy Davenport must have been itching to run their own show at last. After seeing Digger Pugh doing so well down south they would have been expecting to make a considerable profit doing what they did best - promoting. They invested in some pre-race publicity around the city in the local newspapers and promised great things at the stadium. They had also been telling reporters that they had acquired two other venues; Hanley (in Stoke on Trent) and the White City Stadium, Glasgow, up in Scotland.

The Stanley Stadium hadn't seen any stock car racing since the ill-fated meeting of Friday September 24th 1954. During the Grand Final a Rolls Royce collided with another car and then hit the safety fence, bursting through it, and hitting a wall. This incident had killed a 12 year old boy who was watching his father, Ron Smith, taking part.

Vanadore and Davenport clearly weren't superstitious; their opening meeting was on Friday the 13th under the banner of Southern Stock Cars Limited. This wasn't far removed from their name in the States of, Southern Promoters Inc. The Clerk of the course, S.L.Marshall, was actually Les Marshall the promoter from Perry Barr and the Chief lap scorer was listed as Sara Vanadore. Fired with initial optimism they must have been disappointed to find the small 19 car turn-out at their first meeting here in Liverpool.

Heat one was reported as tame, so tame in fact that nobody mentioned the name of the winner and remains, to this day, unknown. Heat two was easily won by Oliver Hart, the ex-speedway rider.

It was time for the all-important international team race. Representing the American team were Bill Irick, Possum Jones, Pete Folse, Bobby Schuyler, Doug (Neil) Castles and Buddy Davenport. The England team comprised of Wilf Blundell, Cyprus Kid, Terry Hill, Harry Marshall, Bill Harrison and Charlie Oates. There was to be a change in the programme schedule as the American team had just lost a race car so Buddy Davenport dropped out and Junior Hart, with his own stock car, became a guest and was racing for the USA.

From the start it began to get physical with both Pete Folse and Bill Irick getting slammed into the fence. However Neil Castles was in fine form and showing his obvious talent. He scored an easy win for the US team with Wilf Blundell scoring a second place for England and the Americans had to rely on Possum jones coming over the line in third place.

Team result; 1st Doug (Neil) Castles USA, 2nd Wilf Blundell

3nd Possum Jones USA, 4th Charlie Oates, 5th Norman Sutton.

Image courtesy of The Liverpool Echo

The USA had won 8 – 7, by the smallest of margins, just one point, but a win is a win all the same. The US team could remain unbeaten for now.

There weren't that many cars left for the Grand Final but those still running were pushed out there to take part. The race started and the small field of cars were doing their best to entertain the crowd. By way of a change the experienced Oliver Hart, an ex-speedway rider from the village of Coppull, near Wigan, was able to beat Neil Castles and get the win. Although someone now questioned just who was driving that USA stock car?

Result; 1st Oliver Hart, 2nd Doug (Neil) Castles USA,

3rd Junior Skarrett, 4th Junior Hart.

Apart from the question of why the managers of the US team decided that Neil Castles would now be known as Doug, which in itself is bizarre, there was another rumour, that the Castles car that came second in the final didn't have Neil (or even Doug!) behind the wheel but an unknown Australian. I would suspect that someone made that simple mistake by not recognising Neil's Carolina accent.

There followed just two days rest and then they were all off on a journey to the West Country and a visit to the Knowle Stadium in Bristol.

The month of May was now getting colder and wetter throughout the whole of the country, bringing out those overcoats and umbrellas. At a Barnsley stock car meeting on May 14th it was pouring with rain, then it started to hail and for a grand finale it began snowing.

Along with the weather going bad, the actual meeting reports coming from some of the local newspapers covering these events were becoming very basic, little more than just the race results, with less racing action being detailed.

Monday May 16th – Knowle Stadium, Bristol.

A reasonable crowd of 6,429 came out and braved the rain to see the American visitors. Things got off to a good start when Possum Jones came first in heat one ahead of Ralph Powell from Bath.

Heat two was won by 'Von Baron', who was really Dick Bradley, the Bristol Speedway rider, in front of second man home Geoff Pymar, another Speedway man. Unfortunately the winner of heat three is another one which has been lost in time and is, at present, unknown with second place going to Eric

Salmon, yet another one of those Speedway riders. The Consolation race followed and was won by Dick Sheppard in his 1937 Chevy.

The Grand Final came round and it was still raining. After a very slippery race the Americans didn't feature anywhere in the placings.

Result; 1st Ralph Powell, 2nd George Staddon, 3rd Cliff Rudrum.

With just one heat win to show for the night at Bristol clearly the American race cars were feeling the strain of the tour and some cars were now more reliable than others plus the Americans weren't used to racing in the rain.

With Bobby Myers shown in the Bristol drivers list, here was another clue that the team had been expecting Bobby to be there. The next day Curtis Crider and Bobby Myers disembarked from the Queen Elizabeth in New York and were off to catch the bus to Greensboro NC.

Friday May 20th – Stanley Stadium, Liverpool.

This was the second stock car meeting to be promoted by Lester Vanadore and Buddy Davenport at the Stanley Stadium. None of the American team members were attending due to their next engagement at Norwich the following day.

There were plenty of crashes and incidents by all accounts. Brian Lennard did a spectacular roll in heat one and was then rammed into the safety fence. He managed to escape from the wreckage despite the roof being crushed and the race was won by Oliver Hart. Then heat two proved to be just as lively when Junior Hart overturned Ben Brown seconds into the race. The race winner was the Manchester based Scot Ian Hastie.

In the Consolation race Reg Spooner was turned on his side by Junior Hart and then, near the end, local man Charlie Oates had a tyre burst and he slid straight into the remains of Spooner's car which put him out of the race. The eventual winner was Wilf Blundell from local man George Woodall. In the last race, the Grand Final, there was no stopping Oliver Hart who raced through the field of cars for the win.

Result; 1st Oliver Hart, 2nd Wilf Blundell, 3rd John Hughes.

Saturday May 21st – The Firs Stadium, Norwich.

The Americans made their first trip to a meeting in East Anglia at Norwich. In the heats the US team members volunteered to start at the back of the grid.

Heat one saw Bobby Schuyler retiring after just one lap and Possum Jones went out four laps later, leaving a local Norwich driver, A.G. Brooks, to race on for the win, with second place going to the Grimsby farmer, John Robinson.

Heat two saw Pete Folse going round in superb form for the win with Possum Jones, who kept going this time, close behind him for second. They were followed home by Bunkey Miles from Great Yarmouth.

In heat three both Castles and Schuyler managed to qualify for the Final after a well-deserved first and second place.

The Consolation race ended in a win for Tony Wickwar from Ipswich.

The Final got underway and Neil Castles showed just how well he could drive to pull off the win. However most eyes were on another driver, local man Len 'Crasher' Allen who was causing all of the thrills and general chaos on track.

Result; 1st Neil Castles USA, 2nd Bill Codling, 3rd George Foulger.

A pretty good night for some of the team but both Bill Irick and Buddy Davenport didn't get a mention. Were they actually out on the track? Bill Irick wasn't even on the drivers list but Davenport was supposed to be in heat three.

Friday May 27th – Stanley Stadium, Liverpool.

This was Vanadore and Davenport's third meeting in three weeks at the Stanley Stadium and once again the American team were not featured.

Heat one was won by Junior Hart from second man home Ian Hastie ahead of George Woodhall. In heat two Wilf Blundell came through to grab first spot from Charlie Oates then Oliver Hart followed in third place.

Instead of the consolation race there followed a 'Special' race in which Junior Hart managed a win from Wilf Blundell and then Ian Hastie in third. Exactly why it was deemed as 'Special' only Lester Vanadore and Buddy Davenport would know.

The Final was a good race with popular local ace Charlie Oates on top form. Scottish driver Ian Hastie was entertaining the crowd by stopping both Oliver Hart and Junior Hart from getting by. He was driving the less powerful car and his manoeuvring across the track kept them at bay for a while. Each time they attempted to pass he'd veer into them and they would drop back again being careful not to be taken out.

Junior Hart then retired from the race and eventually Oliver Hart just disposed of Hastie via the infield to gain third place. Hastie did keep going however, getting fifth place. George Woodhall had already grabbed a third place in his heat and was doing remarkably well as this was only his second race meeting.

Result; 1st Charlie Oates, 2nd George Woodhall,

3rd Oliver Hart, 4th Ron Littler, 5th Ian Hastie.

This was to be the last stock car meeting to be held here at the Stanley Stadium in Liverpool despite Vanadore and Davenport's assurances that they would be back on July 1st with 60 drivers booked in and this would include the return of the American team drivers. They announced that they would then go on to promote on a once a month basis, each meeting being a five event programme.

Luckily the local newspaper, The Liverpool Echo, reported this meeting, as well as the promoters proposed intentions, and published it the very next day. Unfortunately the weekly publication of Speedway & Stock Car World had, for whatever reason, printed this race meeting report (undated) one week late in their June 9th edition. This caused confusion for historians later by suggesting that there was another Liverpool meeting here on Friday June 3rd.

The attendances in Liverpool had not been as good as they had hoped and this meeting was the worst so far; clearly they couldn't make any money here.

Les Marshall meets Davenport, Vanadore, Folse, Irick, and Jones at Perry Barr.

Courtesy of Keith Barber – Stock Car magazine

Chapter Eight – Where is Lester Vanadore?

Saturday May 28th - Perry Barr - Festival of Birmingham Trophy.

Les Marshall was pulling out all the stops on this one, holding a four team event including the Americans. The winners would be awarded the Festival of Birmingham Trophy. But first, to kick things off, The Royal Corps of Signals motorcycle team gave a display of their skills.

Next, an attempt at the flying 2 lap track record from several invited drivers. Robbie Robins was the victor, recording 47 seconds. Then, at last, an actual race was run. Heat one was to be timed at six minutes and was for novice drivers. This resulted in a win for Ed Skeldon with Ivor Hodgkiss in second place and Graham Rowan third.

Heat two was timed at eight minutes and was for seniors. These had all raced in a Perry Barr Final before. This turned out to be far livelier with both Bill Bendix and Phil Hart turning onto their sides and Phil having to help Bill out of his car. The winner was Alan Reader and second man over the line was Wrecker Meadway, who was followed home in third place by Jack Riley.

The next event was the Festival of Birmingham Trophy with four teams lining up and representing London, The Midlands, The North and the USA.

BIRMINGHAM SPEEDWAY, PERRY BARR. 'Phone BIRchfields 6201

WHIT-SATURDAY, 28th MAY, at 7 p.m.

INTERNATIONAL STOCK CAR RACING

FESTIVAL OF BIRMINGHAM TROPHY

with star drivers from U.S.A, London, Midlands
and the North

Display by Royal Corps of Signals' Motor Cycle Team

Grandstand 10/- (bookable); Enclosure 4/- and 3/-, Children 2/-

---

Image courtesy of The Coventry Telegraph

Unfortunately hardly any of the promised Londoners turned up so a last minute team was assembled for them. The Birmingham Trophy race was to be timed at ten minutes.

Another lively race ensued although two of the Americans managed to get through to the front and stayed there until the ten minute limit was reached and so the USA had won the Trophy. The next strongest showing was from the Midland team with the Londoners and the North presumably all being removed by the wrecker trucks.

Result; 1st Pete Folse USA, 2nd Bill Irick USA, 3rd Reg Spooner Midlands,

4th Tatter Meadway Midlands, 5th Bill Bendix Midlands.

The Final was also a ten minute timed event. Once underway, this race saw the Leominster farmer, and on track demolition expert, Bill Bendix out there none the worse for his spill in the second heat. He was physically introducing himself and his chunky stock car to all of the American team and made sure they were in no fit state to win anything! The only USA car to be seen anywhere near the front was Pete Folse. This allowed Reg Spooner a comfortable lead and the large crowd had all enjoyed the show

Result; 1st Reg Spooner, 2nd Allan Reader, 3rd Tatter Meadway,

4th Wrecker Meadway, 5th Pete Folse USA.

Once again the Americans hadn't got the wins that they were used to but they had won the Festival of Birmingham Trophy. Just what state the American stock cars were in after this is anyone's guess but they must have taken some punishment after the ten meetings since arriving here in the UK?

Some of the Americans felt aggrieved as the tactics employed by the opposition had changed from trying to beat them in a race to just trying to stop them. Neil Castles declared that our way of racing was now more like a Demolition Derby! Bobby Schuyler summed things up when he told me, "We were all competitive racers and we soon found out that there was no real competition and we were winning due to having better cars, it was all too easy". True enough, as apart from Johnny Brise, no one else could out race them.

Another 'fly in the ointment,' so to speak, was the fact that since moving out of London the prize money had dried up. Neil Castles explained that Lester Vanadore had told them that, due to the UK currency restrictions, their prize money was being held by Scotland Yard in London.

Obviously they were not happy with this arrangement, especially Neil, the reserve driver in London, as he was now in the main team and had won around £100 of that prize money.

This dubious story of Scotland Yard, home of the London Metropolitan Police, holding on to their cash is implausible as they investigate crimes in the London Boroughs and would have had no jurisdiction for doing so. To this group of American visitors Lester Vanadore's description of the facts would have given Scotland Yard the unquestionable authority, to them, of the FBI.

Unbeknown to Lester Vanadore or Buddy Davenport Buddy Shuman was in contact with Neil Castles, via a weekly phone call, getting an update on how things were going. Clearly Shuman was keeping tabs on Vanadore and the tour.

One of the American team cars was seen out racing again at Belle Vue in Manchester on Wednesday June 1st. However this time there wasn't an American driver behind the wheel. Maybe it was a favour owed by the US team for transport arrangements or maybe a 'try before you buy' scheme? Anyway Jack 'Oily' Wells would have a night of racing a mighty fast car.

Neil Castles with his grey Ford V8 at Perry Barr.

Courtesy of the Neil Castles family collection

Heat one was an easy win for him ahead of John Hughes and the car was to come out again but this time in the hands of Johnny Brise. Johnny had damaged his car in heat two and that was probably all the excuse he needed to pilot the American race car in the Consolation race. This had a large field of 27 cars in the line-up. There were some big names out there too, the likes of Junior Hart and Don Martindale. Although Brise drove fast he was not fast enough to catch the winner, the so called Bruce Blood, real name, John Alexander. He had to make do with second place ahead of Reg Jones.

The Final saw 'Oily' Wells back in the driving seat and showing the field just how fast this car really was during the 20 lap race. He won easily, way ahead of second place man, John Hughes. They were followed home by Ron Hart and Albert Holtby.

At this point of time some of the American drivers had noticed that Lester and Sara Vanadore, along with their Buick, had disappeared and they wanted some answers. The general consensus between them, according to Neil Castles, was that Lester Vanadore had gone to London on business. Buddy Davenport's explanation of their disappearance was that they were in Southampton arranging the team's passage home. Several days passed and there was still no sign of the team's paymaster. They now thought that the missing pair had booked their own passage to New York and gone back home without them.

With the tour finally derailed and heading straight for the buffers they pressed Buddy Davenport for some answers as to what was to happen next, after all, they didn't want to get stranded in a foreign country without the means to return home. Neil Castles still remembers Buddy Davenport reassuring them all and saying that he would to go down to London, visit Scotland Yard, and try to sort out the money that they were owed.

In hindsight Buddy's trip to London wasn't so much to visit Scotland Yard but to liaise with his partner Lester Vanadore. Lester and Sara Vanadore were still very much in this country and didn't leave until the end of June. No doubt they were finalising their plans before leaving. Would Vanadore be trying to sell the six race cars to raise some more cash rather than paying shipping charges?

Buddy Davenport was gone for a day and a half and the US team were relieved when he returned with their passports and tickets to go home to New York on the Queen Elizabeth from Southampton.

Most reports just assumed that the Americans had left via Liverpool but that wasn't possible due to a national dock strike, which now covered the country and sealed up all of the shipping ports. At this time Southampton was the only port getting any ships across the Atlantic, the unions having failed to close it. The Americans must have heard the word 'strike' quite often while they were here as we had a national dock strike, tugboat strike, a railway strike and a newspaper printer's strike and they were only here for a little over nine weeks.

The USA team had raced at ten meetings, the first five while based in London and then five more when based in the Midlands. The three month tour of the UK had turned into a slightly shorter visit. They never got to go up to Scotland as originally planned and, in a strange twist, Wales banned them from racing when big prize money was on offer from the Welsh Mail. The US team cars were deemed not to be proper stock cars by the organisers at Neath Abbey.

Nonetheless the team had flown the Stars & Stripes and had done very well for themselves, winning eleven heats and eight finals between them. They had travelled in the region of 1,500 miles around England and had won all four of the team events at Harringay, Birmingham, Southampton and Liverpool. Bobby Myers had won the Television trophy live on the BBC at Harringay and Possum Jones had won the Sabrina Trophy.

There would have been some unofficial financial rewards for the American promoters, from their UK counterparts, enticing them to visit their own tracks. This was referred to by Curtis Crider as the 'deal money'. The American team had earned around £850 in prize money ($2000). That's worth almost £20,000 today but just how much of that cash actually got through to the drivers is unclear. Neil Castles claims that he never saw a penny of his own prize money.

On Thursday June 9th 1955, aboard the Queen Elizabeth, the remaining team left Southampton without any stock cars or Lester and Sara Vanadore. The White Ghosts, as the American team had become known by the English fans, were presumably glad to be heading back to their familiar homeland.

Neil, a lady passenger, Possum and part of Pete Folse on the Queen Elizabeth.

Courtesy of the Neil Castles family collection

Chapter Nine – The Aftermath

We have to look at what happened next during 1955 to gauge if the American tour had been the cause of more repercussions, on both sides of the Atlantic. Firstly, what was Digger Pugh going to do to get the crowds back to the levels of attendance that he attained during the tour?

Luckily one thing that Digger never had was a shortage of ideas. He decided to organise a stock car World Championship series over a three week period, headlined as the £2,000 Guineas World Championship Trophy. The heats were on June 10th, the Semi-Finals the following week and the Final on June 24th.

Before the Harringay series had even started West Ham announced their own World Championship plans. They wanted to share out the heats and semi-finals to other tracks throughout the country providing, of course, that they could run the World Final at West Ham. This would mean there being two stock car World Champions for 1955. Strangely enough there were two World Champions by the end of the season but West Ham was to play no part in it.

The Harringay World Championship series was a success with Mac McDonnell becoming the new stock car World Champion with the big trophy and £350. On the down side the World Final was to be the last stock car race to be run at Harringay until 1959 and this rather took the gloss off the whole affair. How did this setback come about when, by today's standards, the crowds were still large enough and there was no shortage of cars at Harringay?

It's thought that the Greyhound Racing Association board were reluctant to carry on an association with stock car racing and Digger Pugh as the whole sport by this time was thought to be attracting some unsavoury characters due to the ample cash flow involved and a belief that things weren't being run above-board in some cases. The GRA couldn't afford to tarnish its own credibility due to its betting interests so they decided to end the venture.

Digger must have been taken by surprise by this move but in retrospect maybe he didn't do himself any favours when involving Scotland Yard in his personal affairs and exposing his own 'dirty laundry' to some inspection.

Less than one month after the Harringay closure it was announced that West Ham was to face the same fate and so the whole World Championship plan was shelved. Other big tracks to be closing were Leicester, Coventry and Birmingham, and by the end of the summer things were looking bleak as the novelty was wearing off and crowds were shrinking around the country which had a knock-on effect on the prize money.

Groups of professional drivers began to find it uneconomical to continue their new careers and would have to seek other employment. Bernie Ecclestone had been to Neath Abbey to see the Walker family promoting in Wales and came to the conclusion that it just wasn't viable. After 14 meetings at the Neath Abbey track David Walker agreed and announced its closure having lost in the region of £35,000. Many tracks that had optimistically opened to the sport were now shutting their doors, seeing stock car racing as just a passing craze.

One big track to weather the storm was Belle Vue in Manchester run by the enterprising Johnny Hoskins. He was the promoter to give us a second stock car World Championship race in August, the winner being Jerzy Wojtowicz.

On a more positive note, the many stock car drivers and mechanics that had made their way across the various pit areas at tracks in the spring of '55, to where the US team were encamped, got a closer look at these remarkable race cars and were most impressed by what they saw. Their observations must have helped the trend, in the following seasons, towards the less armoured and lighter cars that would be built more for outright speed.

And as a final footnote, Johnny Brise, the only driver that could actually take on the Americans and on occasion beat them, running his powerful Ardun conversion V8 unit, was to find his engine had become illegal later that year.

Meanwhile, back in the USA.....

Curtis Crawfish Crider had returned with some money but now had no car and Bobby Myers had spent all of his money just getting back home.

His son, Danny Myers, said that when his father turned up on the doorstep he was broke, having spent every last cent on the journey. With a wife and two sons to support and there being no income for the household during his absence they were, for the time being, in a bad place financially.

Whilst Buddy Davenport and the remaining US team members were returning home on the Queen Elizabeth, in Mid-Atlantic, the worst motor racing accident in history was unfolding at the Le Mans 24 hour race in France on June 11th. Almost two and a half hours into the race, at precisely 6.26 pm, a Mercedes hit a bank at the side of the track and disintegrated into a fireball, hurling debris into the crowd. Over 80 spectators were killed and 180 more injured. The race continued while the authorities dealt with the carnage. This disaster caused a shock wave around the world with many calling for a total ban on all forms of motorsport due to the dangers involved.

On Thursday June 14th the team arrived back in New York. It had been eleven weeks since they'd set out from the same pier on the Queen Mary.

Neil Castles returned to Charlotte in North Carolina. He had all of the paperwork to show his boss, Buddy Shuman. This would have shown who raced what and where and also who had used any of the spare parts. Of course now it was totally useless as they had returned without any race cars, without any spare parts, and strangely, without Lester and Sara Vanadore.

Buddy Shuman was quick to get Neil Castles back to work as he had two more race cars to finish building in the workshops, care of the Ford Motor Company, although he was more worried as to the whereabouts of those stock cars he'd supplied for Vanadore's tour. Where the heck was Lester Vanadore anyway? Lester hadn't been seen by the team for several weeks before they'd left England and he wasn't at home: he just seemed to have disappeared.

Speedy Thompson and Buddy Shuman

Courtesy of the Neil Castles family collection

Shuman now felt that he'd run out of options, as well as patience, so he hired lawyers to find Lester Vanadore and his money. Buddy Shuman was still convinced that Vanadore had returned ahead of the team and Buddy Davenport was probably the only person who knew that Lester and Sara Vanadore were still in England.

Lester and Sara Vanadore weren't just sightseeing during their last weeks in the UK as Lester was busy trying to sell all of the tour cars. He was looking for buyers and successfully sold two of them, along with all of the spare parts, to Claude Roe - Roe was promoting at Hednesford with Les Marshall. That would have left four race cars to bring back on the ship and maybe his blue Buick if that wasn't sold as well. On Thursday June 30th Lester and Sara Vanadore boarded the Queen Mary at Southampton; three weeks after the rest of the US team had gone home. They arrived back in New York on Tuesday July 5th and then vanished into a crowded Manhattan.

In August 1955 the American Automobile Association made headlines when they announced that the AAA would no longer sanction any motor racing events. This included the Indianapolis 500. The move cited the Le Mans tragedy and the growing number of racing driver fatalities in the USA.

Around this time detectives found Lester Vanadore living in Nashville Tennessee. He was involved with a Nashville insurance company. Buddy Shuman's lawyers could now finalise the lawsuit.

The NASCAR Grand National season for 1956 was to be a 56 race long series and was to start on November 13th 1955 at Hickory, North Carolina. Buddy Shuman was staying over in a Hickory hotel for the race weekend. Neil Castles states that the court case brought against Lester Vanadore by Shuman was due to be heard before a judge soon after this.

Neil Castles went to see Buddy Shuman on the Saturday night of November 12th. He left him finishing off paperwork in his hotel room around 11 pm. Early the following morning Neil met up with Buddy's brother Frank and was told the awful news that Buddy Shuman, his boss, was dead.

There had been a fire in his hotel room and the fire department had arrived in the early hours of Sunday morning to break down the door. Neil stated that he had been told that Shuman was found with head injuries. It was assumed that he hit his head on a door frame. The local paper detailed the coroner's report; the fireman had found 40 year old Shuman on the floor with the mattress in flames. They added that it looked as though he had tried to get out by mistakenly opening the bathroom door. The cause of death was said to be suffocation by smoke inhalation. Neil added that the fire department didn't carry oxygen on board at that time. The case was finally filed as just another hotel room fire, probably started by a cigarette.

Neil Castles was devastated as he had lost his boss, his friend and his mentor and the case against Lester Vanadore was never heard.

In 1957 the Buddy Shuman Award was created by NASCAR and is awarded annually to individuals or companies whose efforts advance the growth and development of the sport of stock car racing.

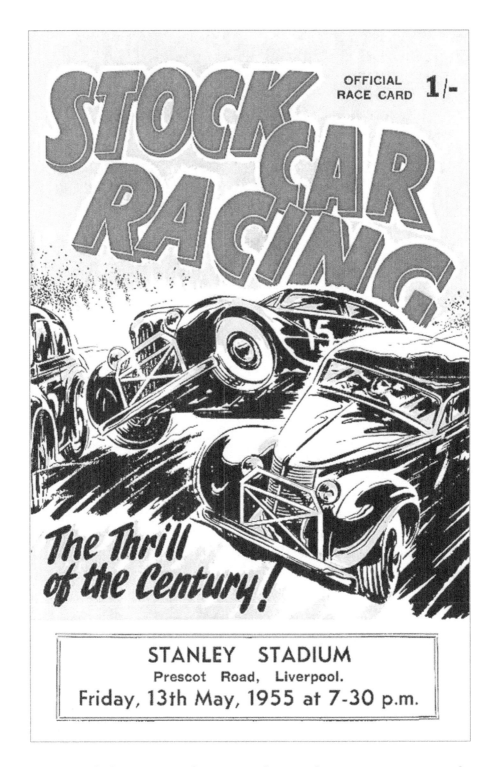

Liverpool, the UK city where Vanadore and Davenport promoted.

The Graham Brown collection

Chapter Ten – What became of the White Ghosts?

What happened to the managers and the seven drivers known as the 'White Ghosts'? The answer was something that I was most interested to find out.

Curtis 'Crawfish' Crider lived in Abbeville, South Carolina and continued in the Modified and Sportsman divisions. A Christmas card received from Johnny Brise in 1956 was just addressed to; Crawfish Crider, South Carolina, USA.

Crider's top flight career in NASCAR was from 1959 until 1965 in the Grand National division where he enjoyed seven seasons, being ranked 6th during his best year in 1964. He subsequently moved to the Florida coast at Ormond Beach and English stock car racer Pete Tucker and his family became regular visitors. After Curtis retired from racing he started co-promoting at some of the local raceways in Florida before running an asphalting business for a while. In 1987 he wrote a book covering his racing career, *The Road to Daytona*. Eventually he opened his own vehicle restoration workshop. Curtis 'Crawfish' Crider died in December 2012 aged 82.

Bobby Harris Myers was Curtis Crider's amigo on the early voyage home in 1955. Bobby and his brother Billy were regular racers at the Bowman Gray Stadium in Winston-Salem, North Carolina, where they both became track champions. They enjoyed regular rivalry with another race car driver, Curtis Turner. Both Billy and Bobby were working-class mechanics driving their own cars but Turner was a flash playboy who drove cars belonging to other people. If Turner wrecked his race car, or that of anyone else, he wasn't that bothered. Turner's attitude got to the Myers brothers; clearly they were going to clash. Several races turned into three way demolition derbies after things got heated. The promoter knew it kept the fans coming back so encouraged the feud.

Bobby had started in a few Grand National races in 1951. He drove part time in the series and was ranked 29th in 1954. In the 1955 season, when Bobby had his brief vacation in England, his brother Billy finished the year as National Champion of the Sportsman Division.

During the Southern 500 race at Darlington, on September 2nd 1957, Fonty Flock spun at the end of the back straight and was parked sideways on turn 3. Bobby Myers and Paul Goldman both slammed into the stopped car at full speed. All three suffered serious injuries and although Flock and Goldman survived the crash Bobby Myers died soon after reaching hospital. He was just 30 years old.

Bobby's Television Trophy was later sent over to Laura Myers, his widow, from Bill Cook in London.

In April 1958 his brother, Billy Myers, suffered a heart attack during a Modified race at the Bowman-Gray Stadium and died: he was only 33 years of age.

The National Motorsports Press Association annually presents the Myers Brothers Memorial Award to the person or company that has contributed most to the sport of stock car racing during that year.

Bobby's son, Danny 'Chocolate' Myers, grew up to become the Gasman in the Flying Aces NASCAR pit crew of Richard Childress and seven time NASCAR Winston Cup Series Champion, Dale Earnhardt. Even today, long after their premature demise, the older fans at the Bowman Gray Stadium still regard Bobby and Billy Myers as racing legends.

William Luther Irick has not set the record books alight but no doubt enjoyed his racing. Curtis Crider recalled the time when Bill was lined up to race a fast new stock car that Curtis liked the look of. Curtis got the owner to let him race it instead, thereby pushing Irick out of a drive. He then let Bill race his own stock car at the meeting. Crider watched Irick racing his car in heat one and during the race Bill accidently smashed into a two car wreck ahead of him and damaged Crider's race car for him. Curtis did get to drive the new car until they repaired his old one.

Bill Irick was a US Army veteran in the 82nd Airborne Division and was an avid fisherman and hunter. When Bill finished his racing career he become a Millwright but retired after an accident. William Luther Irick died in September 2001 aged 71 in Wilmington NC.

Lewis 'Possum' Jones raced in the NASCAR Grand National series on a part time basis in the 1950s and 1960s. His first race was the 1952 Southern 500 at Darlington, South Carolina. Jones had his longest season in 1960, with 13 starts and ranked 13th. He was also one of the original drivers to compete in the NASCAR Convertible division which ran from 1956. Here he managed 2 wins and 20 top five places. In 1963 and 1964 'Possum' became a NASCAR race car owner. His final race was 1965 at the Daytona 500 in Florida. He died in Okeechobee, Florida in December 1997 aged 63.

Ansley Peter Folse is thought to have been born in New Orleans in 1925. He never knew his father or his actual date of birth. He started his career by racing motorcycles in California during 1949.

Always known as Pete, he was arguably, to become the most successful driver of the group. He began racing Sprint cars and in the early 1950s, changed tack to become a top Modified stock car driver in Florida.

After his trip to England he went back to the Sprint car dirt tracks and got his big break in 1959. With the retirement of Bobby Grim, Hector Honore chose Folse as the replacement pilot for his Bardahl Special 'Black Deuce' Sprint car. Pete Folse won three IMCA (International Motor Contest Association) Sprint Car Championships in a row, 1959, 1960 and 1961. He followed that up with two consecutive runners up places in 1962 and 1963, and was known as 'The Flying Frenchman'. The Mayor of Tampa was so pleased with all of the good publicity brought to his home town that he announced a 'Pete Folse Day'.

Hector Honore and Pete Folse win another trophy with the 'Black Deuce'.

Courtesy of the Abraham Lincoln Presidential Library and Museum

Pete retired from racing but suffered with bad health in his later years and died in September 1975, aged 50. Pete Folse is to be found listed in the National Sprint Car Hall of Fame, Knoxville, Iowa.

Henry Neil 'Soapy' Castles began his racing career as a young lad entering a soap box derby competition. Buddy Shuman helped him build it and christened him Soapy after the Police had caught him speeding down the road with it. Later he raced in Midget cars, Sprint cars and Stock cars and then entered the NASCAR Convertible race division. He started in the top Grand National and Winston Cup series from 1957 through to 1976. He gained 51 top five finishes and 178 top ten finishes.

Neil Castles began an affiliation with Hollywood as a stuntman in the movie Thunder Road in 1958, so for a while he was both a racer and a stuntman. In 1967 he drove the film car out on track for the Elvis Presley movie, Speedway, which also starred Nancy Sinatra.

Neil retired from racing but continued his film and TV work into the 1990s. He bought some land to extend his truck repair business and, along with several of the local townspeople, he became very unwell. Exxon had been repairing aircraft re-fuelling tankers on the site and had contaminated the ground water with leaking fuel. The toxins in the drinking water caused some nasty illnesses in the local population. Neil himself lost an eye and now had lung damage.

Neil Castles and his wife Jean filed a case against Exxon in 1995 and went to court. Despite a jury awarding them $500,000 the judge stated that the evidence did not support the jury's award. The Castles appealed and the settlement was eventually reinstated in 2000.

I was lucky enough to speak to him on the phone and my intended ten minute call lasted an hour; he still had plenty of memories regarding the tour. At the time of writing Neil Castles is 86 years of age and lives in North Carolina.

Bobby Crowson Schuyler was by far the hardest of the group to find and although his name is mentioned in the NASCAR record books, the details were scant to say the least. In 1964 he completed 3 laps of the Islip raceway NY: one race with his location and age unknown.

Knowing that he was living in Rock Hill, South Carolina in 1955 I looked at the US census for 1940 to see if there was a Robert Schuyler in the right age group in South Carolina and that's when I found him at 4 years old. I traced him to an address in Florida and wrote to him but got no reply. I later found a phone number and rang it and waited. I was relieved when the phone was picked up and a voice with a strong Southern accent answered and then agreed that he was on the tour. Bobby hadn't received my earlier letter because he had recently moved. We got talking about the tour and I rang him a couple of times.

Bobby was the son of a Coca-Cola employee and was the youngest of the team of American drivers in 1955, being only 19 at the time. His memory of the tour isn't that clear these days, as he says, "It was a long time ago."

Bobby remembers Digger Pugh and who wouldn't! Bobby vividly remembers visiting a restaurant across from the Harringay Arena and the lady owner would make him a wonderful iced tea (a beverage difficult to find in London during 1955). After finding himself a minor celebrity in the restaurant he was taken on a sightseeing tour of London by several of her friends.

Once Bobby returned to the USA he became a qualified mechanic and drove in in Modified races. In 1959, when Curtis Crider entered the NASCAR Grand National division, Bobby had helped him to prepare the race car. His big break came in 1964 when Ray Fox wanted him to drive his Dodge stock car in a NASCAR Winston Cup race at Islip Raceway NY. Unfortunately the car broke down after 3 laps. Ray Fox was a good friend of his but he never got to race the car again. In the same race at Islip Curtis Crider stopped with steering problems after 139 laps and Neil Castles finished in 6th place after running the full 300 laps.

At the time of writing Bobby Schuyler is 85 years old and lives in Florida.

The Television Trophy won by Bobby Myers at Harringay.

Courtesy of Caron and Danny Myers – oldstox.com

Chapter Eleven – Promoter Tales

Let's start with that little guy with the big charisma, John W. L. Pugh.

Digger Pugh, as he always seemed to be known, has had so much written and said about him over the years that it's hard to see through the showbiz exterior and find the real person. Some accounts of how he reached Australia, by emigrating from England with his parents when young, sound straight forward at first. The problem being that their move from Kingsthorpe in Northampton to Australia was a little exaggerated as they had only moved across the town of Northampton! Digger's parents, John and Eleanor Pugh, spent from 1899 until 1921 enlarging their family in Northampton, having nine children. This would make Digger's story more feasible and is corroborated by his son Johnny.

Digger tells of making his own way to Australia and this is where his total commitment to impress other people seems to stem from. He wrote home but was desperate to show them how successful he had become. If nothing else he had to be resilient and a survivor to overcome all the hardships a young runaway would encounter, and obviously had a sense of adventure.

We have already covered, in chapter two, his incredible life up until 1955 which is documented and verified by others but there was another Pugh, the one who would mix true facts with fiction and embroider these tall tales in order to increase his stature and impress other people.

John Pugh's claim to have joined the Australian Imperial Forces during WW1 is not all it seems. Graeme Hosken, editor of 'Digger', the Australian magazine for most things connected to the AIF during WW1, confirmed that John W.L. Pugh had never enlisted. However Pugh did register for work in an Australian munitions factory and joined the AIF recruitment drive in 1917. Tales of Pugh as a 13 or 14 year old bugler on the Western Front being gassed and wounded were part of the speech he gave at the recruitment meetings. Did it really happen just as he described it or did he have a vivid imagination?

Was he a Flight Lieutenant in Iraq and a flying ace in WW1 before his 16th birthday or is that another story to impress the folks back home? His son, Johnny Pugh, remembers a letter being delivered to the house in Hounslow addressed to William Peter Boulton Pugh MBE. Digger told him that he had used the name and identity of William Peter Boulton Pugh to increase his age by four years and join the RAF in 1917. He also told his son that he was awarded the MBE as his Squadron flew a record number of flights, carrying food and supplies, to a beleaguered regiment who were cut off by the Turks in Mesopotamia, now Iraq. Strange as it may seem, his actual tale of the regiment that was cut off by Ottoman forces during WW1 and flown food supplies by air is actually true. Unfortunately it happened in April 1916, before the RAF was formed and before young John W.L. Pugh had even left England.

Digger Pugh may have actually found the name of William Peter Boulton Pugh MBE in the 1919 Military Honours list. This huge list of 10,000 names being awarded for their war service was printed as a supplement of the London Gazette in most of the newspapers at the time throughout the Empire. Finding a Pugh with an MBE may have been too good to be true for Digger.

The war record of the real William Peter Boulton Pugh shows that he was promoted to 2nd Lieutenant in the RAF and awarded the MBE in 1919 for his war service and that he had a family in Alberta where he worked for the Canadian government. He was an English-born Canadian. Digger Pugh was so impressed with William that he decided to start going by the name of the Canadian. In the 1930s he travelled under the name of William Pugh on a British passport.

In 1927 Digger returned home to Northampton, aged 24, for the first time since he had run away and, with his letters home, was thought of as a war hero and a champion boxer by his family. Knowing the importance of publicity he called in at the Northampton newspaper offices to let them know of his many accomplishments and sporting feats and soon the local paper ran the story, DIGGER PUGH BACK HOME, NORTHAMPTON FLY-WEIGHT WHO BOXED PANCHO VILLA.

His story of fighting the world flyweight boxing champion the previous August was impossible as Pancho Villa had died in 1925. Digger Pugh was a professional flyweight boxer in Australia between 1922 and 1929 but again, being desperate to impress, he told people that he was the undefeated Australian Flyweight champion. A quick check in the record books will reveal that he was not. In fact he only had seven professional fights between 1922 and 1929 and he failed to win any of them.

Although only a whisker over five feet and one inch tall Pugh was of a stocky build and very fit through his boxing training and being an acrobat. His constant need to impress carried on throughout his life, not least when he met with NASCAR officials in Florida and told them of his many sporting feats.

After being practically evicted from Harringay in 1955 he began to lose interest in stock cars and drifted back to his talent agency.

Digger's later years became an arduous battle with cancer until his death on February 1st 1969, aged 66. Ironically his friend and Harringay Circus associate, Tom Arnold, died the very next day.

Digger Pugh is remembered far more in circus and theatre folklore than for his brief involvement in the UK stock car scene in the 1950s. Despite his shortcomings he would always give praise to you for a good job and likewise be as quick to tell you when he was displeased. Being such a showman his greatest attribute was that he knew how to entertain an audience, be that in a stadium, a theatre or a circus ring and he brought great joy and excitement into many people's lives over the years.

Buddy Davenport worked with several promoters but was working alongside Lester Vanadore at the time of the tour in 1955. Taking a wild guess I would suspect that Mr Davenport preferred to be called Buddy rather than his real first name of Cuthbert. Buddy was always the P.A. announcer at the stadium and could get the crowd buzzing with his rousing commentaries.

His friend Curtis Crider tells of the time when Buddy forgot his stopwatch. This would be needed to time each entrant before the race meeting and get a timed lap for their starting positions. Not wishing to disappoint the fans and drivers alike, he improvised. Buddy sat there hanging out of his kiosk window holding the stopwatch and apparently timing each car. He made sure he over emphasised the starting and stopping of the watch. But he was only holding a silver dollar coin in his hand. No one was close enough to notice so he just guessed all of their times. The strange thing was that nobody disputed his timing as sometimes happened when he used the real stopwatch. Now that's a true showman for you.

When he returned from the tour we assume it was business as usual even with his co-promoter Lester Vandadore moving away. In the late 1950s he made a success of transforming several abandoned minor league baseball parks into motor speedways. Buddy also had his day job selling cars and trucks at the local Chevrolet dealership in Charlotte, North Carolina. Buddy Davenport died at his home in Charlotte in 1980 at the age of 62.

William, Lester, Vanadore is last on the list but he had lead just as complex a life as any of the others. Neil Castles says that his last recollection of seeing Lester Vanadore was at Buddy Shuman's funeral service in 1955 when he showed up in a brand new white Cadillac. Obviously there was a slight misunderstanding as to whether Vanadore actually owed Shuman any money. It would seem that Neil Castles and Buddy Shuman both thought that he did, perhaps Lester Vanadore himself thought otherwise.

Buddy Shuman's enquiries had found Lester Vanadore working and living in Nashville so that appeared to be the place to start the search.

In 1956 the name Lester Vanadore comes to light in a report by the US Securities and Exchange Commission. The SEC was investigating a proposed share issue that Lester Vanadore was involved in. A group of businessmen were trying to raise $8,000,000 with shares in a new Nashville company within the insurance field. The SEC had become concerned as the proposal contained, as they put it, misleading statements and omissions.

One of the proposers was Hubert Long who was an important name in the country music industry. Another, Frank Poole, was an attorney in Nashville. The Commission was also unhappy with the inexperience of Lester Vanadore, an ex-stock car promoter, and T. Fontell Flock who was none other than 'Fonty' Flock the stock car driver. The Commission issued a Stop Order on the venture.

Moving onto 1963, there was another share issue looked into by the US Securities and Exchange Commission, this time for a company formed that year for recording, distributing and publishing music. The company needed to raise 297,000 shares and build their own headquarters with two recording studios in Nashville. One of the directors was Hubert Long and the two vice presidents were Frank Poole and Lester Vanadore: the same three associates were looking to raise funds on a new venture. They were all cleared by the SEC and Lester Vanadore later became the Company President and he also went on to become a successful Nashville TV producer.

Just what was going on when the tour ended, had Lester Vanadore suffered a mid-life crisis in 1955/56 and run away to Nashville?

It seems that Lester was indeed a genuine country music fan and co-wrote several songs while he was in Nashville. *Google* Lester Vanadore today and you will find him credited with co-writing and arranging many country music songs. He became one of the cogs in the Nashville music machine, but that only spanned the last 22 years of his life, the first 33 years seem to have just been forgotten along with his association with Buddy Davenport and NASCAR.

William Lester Vanadore died in Nashville on November 2nd 1978. He was aged 55 and was buried back in South Carolina, along with his past.

Chapter Twelve - Loose Ends

This is the last piece of the story, where we'll tie up some of the loose ends.

The infamous Crawfish Crider stock car was repaired and Digger Pugh got the racer Percy Betts to drive it for him. Percy Betts raced the car in the Harringay World Final in June 1955 and he managed a third place finish after starting right at the back of the grid.

Claude Roe, the promoter who purchased two race cars from Lester Vanadore, put them up for sale in 1956. The grey Neil Castles Ford model 40 was bought by Allen Briggs and Johnny Brise bought the Bobby Myers model 78 car. Johnny Brise drove the car successfully to become World Champion at Belle Vue and the first national points champion in 1956.

The expected three month American tour of the UK had ended up being a tour of England split into two halves and had only lasted two months. Johnny Pugh said that after the first few meetings Digger Pugh had planned a trip over to the continent to race the US team in France. Was this why, in the first Harringay race programme, it wished the team a warm welcome and hoped that they would always have very pleasant recollections of their first European tour? The team were quick to move on as soon as the three promoters fell out. Vanadore and Davenport must have been sure they could make more money going elsewhere while over here but that seems not to have worked out.

We have wandered through the Southern States and seen where stock car racing began. We now know who those American racers and promoters were, to some degree, and we have also discovered what became of them after the tour. It scarcely seems possible today that the British stock car scene was ever affiliated to NASCAR and Bill France but it was, however briefly.

I hope you also got an idea how things were living in a 1950s Britain. The UK stock car scene back then was a new phenomenon; after years of shortages and rationing it brought some fun back to ordinary people's lives. Thousands flocked to get a glimpse of those crazy cars and the men and women who, for the most part, never would have considered being budding racing drivers but for the likes of Digger Pugh, who made it all possible.

The whole sport at the beginning was like a balloon being pumped up, it could only go so far before it would burst, and it was at its peak, or thereabouts, when the Americans sailed through on their tour.

When the 1956 and 1957 seasons came around things had moved on and as usual no one wanted to listen to reason until they had their backs to the wall. In a climate of doom and gloom things needed to change. The 1955 season finished with a record 238 meetings at 46 different tracks. By the end of 1957, this had dropped to 99 meetings at 20 tracks, the sport having been decimated by both waning public interest and the unfortunately timed Suez crisis with all of its consequences.

Luckily people like Peter Arnold, Digger Pugh's old general manager, came forward with some smart ideas and got people working together. In came a national numbering system, roof grades and reverse grids and many more improvements. They had already formed the British Stock Car Drivers Association (BSCDA) and now all of the rival promoters could work together and plan ahead within the British Stock Car Association (BriSCA). The sport would be able to evolve and adapt as it climbed out of the 1950s and gained new fans throughout the coming decades. Although, to be fair to those old racing pioneers of 1955, getting 40,000 plus spectators into a stadium to watch stock car racing in this country is unlikely to ever be repeated.

As a final farewell I would like to thank Bobby Schuyler for teaching me, and anyone reading this book for that matter, three important things during our phone calls. First, that Schuyler is pronounced Skyler, not Shyler, second that Folse is pronounced Folls, not Folssie and last, that ice cold tea *is* drinkable!

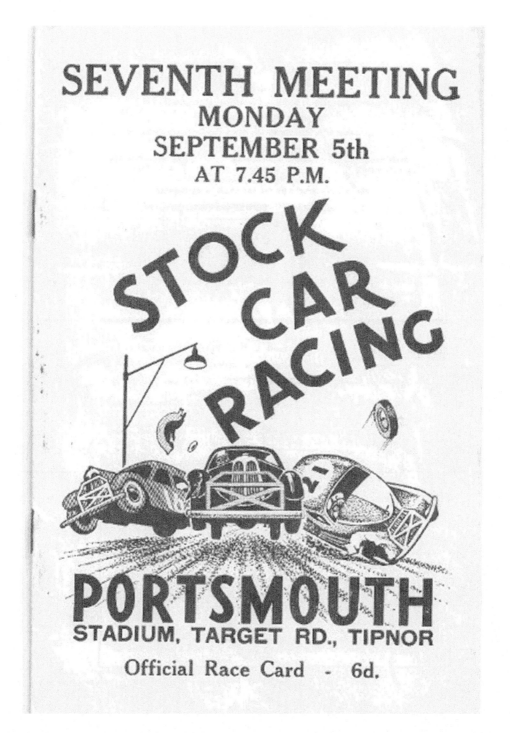

Some UK towns and cities saw stock car racing as just a passing craze.

The Graham Brown collection

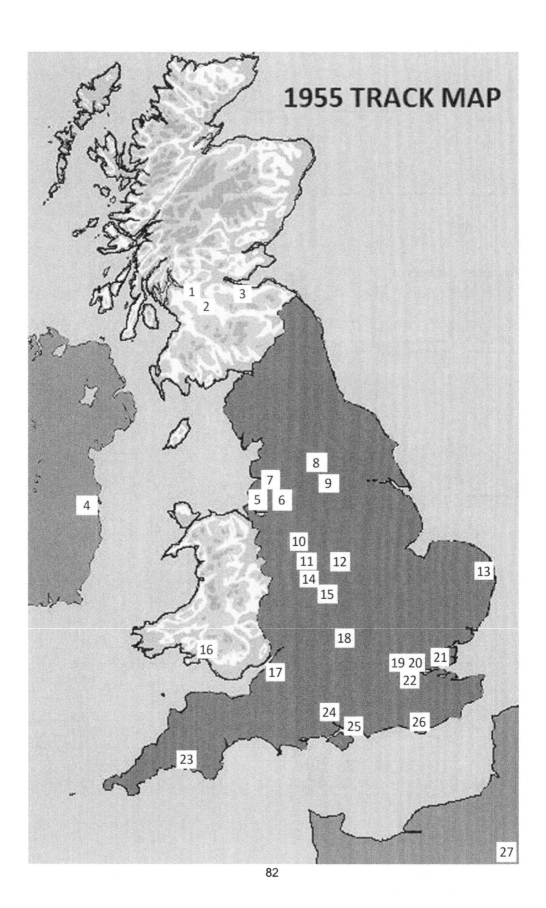

1955 TRACK MAP

Track locations

For anyone who is unaccustomed to our geography, or just for general interest, these are where all of the 1955 tracks mentioned in this book were located. Sadly very few of these old venues still exist today.

1. White City Stadium, Glasgow.
2. Motherwell Stadium.
3. Meadowbank Stadium, Edinburgh.
4. Shelbourne Park, Dublin.
5. Stanley Stadium, Liverpool.
6. Belle Vue Stadium, Manchester.
7. Cuerden Park, Preston.
8. Odsal Stadium, Bradford
9. Queen's Ground Raceway, Barnsley.
10. Hanley Stadium, Stoke-on-Trent.
11. Hednesford Hills Stadium, Cannock.
12. Leicester Stadium.
13. The Firs Stadium, Norwich.
14. Perry Barr Stadium, Birmingham.
15. Coventry Stadium.
16. Neath Abbey Raceway.
17. Knowle Stadium, Bristol
18. Cowley Stadium, Oxford.
19. Harringay Stadium, London.
20. Custom House Stadium, West Ham, London.
21. Weir Stadium, Rayleigh.
22. New Cross Stadium, London
23. Plymouth Sports Stadium, Pennycross, Plymouth.
24. Bannister Court Stadium, Southampton.
25. Portsmouth Sports Stadium, Target Road, Portsmouth
26. Arlington Raceway, Eastbourne.
27. Buffalo Stadium, Paris.

The US Team's Tour Timeline

- April 5th   US team arrive in Southampton.

- April 8th   First International match held at Harringay.

- April 10th   Three of the team race at Arlington, Eastbourne.

- April 16th   TV Trophy qualifying heats held at Harringay.

- April 20th   Curtis Crider races at Belle Vue, Manchester.

- April 23rd   TV Trophy held at Harringay.

- April 29th   Second International match held at Southampton.

- May 4th   Curtis Crider and Bobby Myers head for home.

- May 7th   Third International match held at Perry Barr.

- May 13th   Fourth International match held at Liverpool.

- May 16th   US team race at Bristol.

- May 21st   US team race at Norwich.

- May 28th   Festival of Birmingham Trophy at Perry Barr.

- June 9th   Buddy Davenport and the US team leave for home.

- June 30th   Sara and Lester Vanadore leave for home.

About the Author

Born in 1951, I was brought up in the monochrome world of 1950s London. I can still remember my first visit to Harringay Stadium when I was ten years old and catching that stock car bug, for which there is no known cure. I began having fun on the track myself, racing Bangers from 1973 until 1976. The following season I decided to upgrade to the Spedeworth Superstox but after five months I felt that both car and driver weren't up to the competition. I became more interested in the pioneers of the sport in both the US and the UK and was fascinated to read about just how much the sport has evolved and diversified over time. That initial stock car explosion ignited by Digger Pugh in 1954 came a few years too early for me to fully appreciate. However, being retired now, I think I have absorbed the atmosphere through the many hours of research on the subject combined with my own memories of 1950s London.

Me and the pink Minx after a Destruction Derby at Aldershot Stadium in 1976.

Claude Roe selling the stock cars he bought from Lester Vanadore.

Courtesy of Keith Barber – Stock Car magazine

Bibliography

Reference Books and Articles

The US of A White Ghost Team (Stock Car magazine 2011) by Keith Barber.

Brisca Formula One (1954-2004) by Keith Barber and Malc Aylott.

Neil Soapy Castles: Memoir of a Life in NASCAR and the Movies

by Neil Soapy Castles with Perry Allen Wood.

The Road to Daytona by Curtis Crider and Don O'Reilly.

Forty Years of Stock Car racing – Volume One by Greg Fielden.

Real NASCAR by Daniel S. Pierce.

The Digger Pugh Girls by Don Stacey.

The Story of Stock car Racing (1954/55) by Keith and Glenys Thompson.

The Thrill of the Century by Pete Tucker.

The US Securities and Exchange Commission (reports 1956-1957 & 1963).

Bernie by Susan Watkins.

Beryl Howlett, My Life as an Acrobat by Lyn Wilton.

John W.L.Pugh with Private Stuart at a recruitment drive for
The Australian Imperial Forces in 1917.

Courtesy of Graeme Hosken – Digger magazine

My diorama of Bobby Myers receiving the TV Trophy in 1/32 scale.

If you have enjoyed reading this please add your book review on Amazon to improve its profile and, in turn, help us to raise more funds for the charity.

Front cover design – Steve Daily – photo courtesy of Keith Barber

Printed in Great Britain
by Amazon